"Bringing his lifetime of grappling faithfully with all things Buechner, the inestimable Jeff Munroe proves a winsome and trustworthy guide to the essential works of Frederick Buechner. If you've always wanted to read Buechner but didn't know where to start, *Reading Buechner* is the introduction you've been looking for. And if you're a longtime reader, Jeff does a lovely job of finding new ways to appreciate and celebrate the richness of Buechner's works."

Jennifer L. Holberg, Calvin University professor of English and codirector, Calvin Center for Faith & Writing

"I am one who wonders why so many Christians spend so much time talking about and writing about Christianity. Instead of the Word becoming flesh, it becomes more and more words. Jeffrey Munroe, in his masterfully clear and insightful *Reading Buechner*, opens up about why Frederick Buechner devoted his career to, yes, more words. Why? Because incarnation is at the heart of Buechner's faith. His great hope is that his words, like all effective literature, will become flesh, in his work Christian flesh. Munroe, in a voice that feels as if he is sitting with you on the porch, reveals that Buechner writes out from the 'flesh' of his inner life hoping to connect with the inner life of anyone struggling within God's love-endangered world. Even if you've already read Buechner's work, read Jeffrey Munroe's informative and invigorating *Reading Buechner*, then get on it and read Buechner again, perhaps for the first time."

Jack Ridl, author of *Broken Symmetry, Losing Season, Practicing to Walk Like a Heron,* and *St. Peter and the Goldfinch*

"Jeff has listened to the depth and more significantly to the breadth of Buechner's work in a way no one else ever has. His work enables each of us now to listen further to Buechner's remarkable literary voice for ourselves. Moreover, this book comes at a crucial time, providing the next generation with a badly needed introduction to one of the most important theological writers of our time."

Michael Card, Bible teacher, songwriter

"With a personal appreciation for Frederick Buechner's words and a thoroughly researched knowledge of the experiences that formed them, Jeffrey Munroe's *Reading Buechner* is a deft combination of biography and reading companion. I had only known Buechner from *Telling the Truth*; this book has inspired me to seek out so much more."

Josh Larsen, author of *Movies Are Prayers* and editor/podcast host for *ThinkChristian*

"*Reading Buechner* gives us exactly what the title promises. These are a fan's notes, based on many years of reading and reflection, aimed at fellow Buechnerites but also readily accessible to newcomers. Unpretentious but deeply versed in his subject, Jeffrey Munroe is a winsome guide."

John Wilson, contributing editor, *Englewood Review of Books*

"A much-needed spiritual biography of the minister-writer who has found himself walking the borders (to quote visual artist Makoto Fujimura) of faith and literature, never truly at home in either. Jeffrey Munroe invites us to listen not only to Frederick Buechner's books but also to his life. And in turn, we listen to our own."

Sarah Arthur, author of *A Light So Lovely*

"These lively reflections on Buechner's writing and life, laced with well-told anecdotes and theological insights, offer readers a valuable guide and a capacious story of grace. Jeff Munroe brings his own considerable skill in storytelling, his deeply informed admiration for a monumental life and work, and his deep faith to bear on the happy task of helping the rest of us read Buechner—with fresh appreciation for the way he continues to speak into a new historical moment with truths that emerge 'from below time.'"

Marilyn McEntyre, author of *Caring for Words in a Culture of Lies* and *Word by Word*

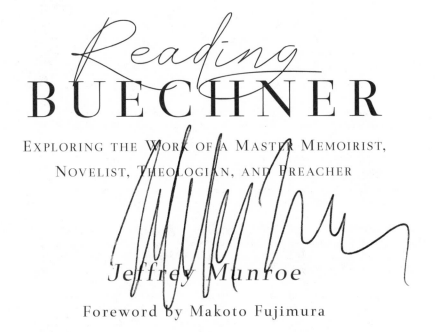

Reading
BUECHNER

EXPLORING THE WORK OF A MASTER MEMOIRIST, NOVELIST, THEOLOGIAN, AND PREACHER

Jeffrey Munroe

Foreword by Makoto Fujimura

An imprint of InterVarsity Press
Downers Grove, Illinois

InterVarsity Press
P.O. Box 1400, Downers Grove, IL 60515-1426
ivpress.com
email@ivpress.com

*InterVarsity Press® is the book-publishing division of InterVarsity Christian Fellowship/USA®, a
movement of students and faculty active on campus at hundreds of universities, colleges, and schools
of nursing in the United States of America, and a member movement of the International Fellowship
of Evangelical Students. For information about local and regional activities, visit intervarsity.org.*

Cover design: Cindy Kiple
Interior design: Jeanna Wiggins
Images: photo of Frederick Buechner by Blake Gardner / Wikimedia Commons

ISBN 978-0-8308-4580-4 (print)
ISBN 978-0-8308-5314-4 (digital)

Printed in the United States of America ∞

Library of Congress Cataloging-in-Publication Data
A catalog record for this book is available from the Library of Congress.

P 25 24 23 22 21 20 19 18 17 16 15 14 13 12 11 10 9 8 7 6 5 4 3 2 1

Y 38 37 36 35 34 33 32 31 30 29 28 27 26 25 24 23 22 21 20 19

FOR GRETCHEN, AMANDA,

AND JESSE

CONTENTS

FOREWORD

Makoto Fujimura

THE FIRST LINES OF JEFF MUNROE'S REFLECTION on Frederick Buechner's work take the reader into Jeff's sudden traumatic journey with his twenty-four-year-old fiancée. The immediacy of his recollections brought me back to the forlorn, trauma-filled days after 9/11. In my loft in downtown Manhattan, barely three blocks away from Ground Zero, I was trying to cope with the losses of our neighborhood and neighbors, and trying to find the normalcy of daily rhythm for our children. We weren't allowed back home until Thanksgiving, and in the ensuing months, after our adrenaline rush had disappeared, I remember the emptiness of the vacuous, vacant hole in the sky and the acrid smell of the air. Ground Zero was my home, and my children had become "Ground Zero children."

One evening during those fear-filled, uncertain days, I was writing in my home office when I noticed a book that I had placed on a small shelf in front of me: Frederick Buechner's *The Longing for Home*. I had placed the book there, partly because it was well-designed (unusual for a "Christian author" back then), among other well-designed items I liked (such as a Van Gogh baseball I bought at the Met Museum gift shop that made me smile). Now I began to reread

Buechner and began my deeper journey with the content of a book of "midlife reflection," which became a map for my post-9/11 fog-filled days.

The irony here is that I was "home," but I was yet longing for one. Buechner's eloquence is unmatched:

> The world floods in on all of us. The world can be kind, and it can be cruel. It can be beautiful, and it can be appalling. It can give us good reason to hope and good reason to give up all hope. It can strengthen our faith in a loving God, and it can decimate our faith. In our lives in the world, the temptation is always to go where the world takes us, to drift with whatever current happens to be running strongest. When good things happen, we rise to heaven; when bad things happen, we descend to hell. When the world strikes out at us, we strike back, and when one way or another the world blesses us, our spirits soar. I know this to be true of no one as well as I know it to be true of myself. . . . The fragmentary nature of our experience shatters us into fragments. Instead of being whole, most of the time we are in pieces, and we see the world in pieces, full of darkness at one moment and full of light the next.[1]

The last two lines of this paragraph opened me up like a sharp surgeon's knife.

As an artist, I employ the *nihonga* method (literally "Japanese style painting"). The materials used for this method are pulverized minerals. At the *nihonga* pigment shop, artisans pulverize minerals such as malachite and azurite by hand, so they develop a refractive quality that I then layer onto a surface of paper. The resulting layers are prismatic, creating not just blue and green but rainbow hues. In Buechner's writing, and now with Jeff Munroe's guidebook for understanding Buechner deeply, there are pulverized rainbow hues that help us see into our lives as well. We can find true beauty in pulverization. And we can see the full spectrum of colors through a world in pieces, especially if you live in a home called "Ground Zero."

Furusato, a Japanese term for home, literally means "old country." It's the place that you have grown up in. For my children, *furusato* will forever be Ground Zero. What it means for them to "come home" is different in a post-9/11 world, and yet their longing for a true home is still there. What Fredrick Buechner focuses on, which Jeff highlights in this book, is that such a journey of longing is defined individually by unique markers, real faces and real names, refracted through the brokenness of a shattered world. They are signposts of a greater reality to come, and they fill us with grace, laughter, disappointment, and new desires. The vacant hole in the sky, too, will be replenished with new buildings, but our hearts will always be "longing for home," because our fragmentary lives will push us to people, communities, and ultimately a New Country.

"Home" will have particular faces: for Jeff it is Gretchen; for Buechner, it's Naya, Godric, Bebb, Brendan, and Judy, to name a few, and of course, his daughters, and his father, who committed suicide when Buechner was a boy. We hear their voices, and their stories refract beautifully. Buechner makes them fully present, generously inviting us into their world. Buechner's eloquence, his theological acumen, and his poetic nuances are ultimately brought into illuminating the people in the communities and families he has endeavored to uphold. Jeff's gift to us gives us a glimpse into the vast, rich arena of Buechner's offerings, a kind of a kaleidoscopic capturing that is mesmerizing to peek into, and gives light to each broken piece of their sacred stories. We all have been pulverized in some way, and the layers of these prismatic stories are worth beholding, even in a place called "Ground Zero."

INTRODUCTION
How Reading Buechner Changed My Life

O NE JULY AFTERNOON IN 1985, a month before our wedding, my twenty-four-year-old fiancée suffered a massive stroke.

I was housesitting in my hometown of Holland, Michigan, minding both a house and a high school student whose parents were away for a week, and my fiancée, Gretchen, had promised to make us dinner that evening. The high school student and I were both sacked out on his family room couches while Harry Caray droned on about the Cubs. When Gretchen came in from work, we barely moved except to give her a hard time about waking us up. A moment later she called to me from the bathroom. I'm not sure why I got right up, given that we'd just been goofing around, but something in her voice gave me the idea that I should. I found her standing in the bathroom with a ribbon of drool dropping down from the left side of her mouth. A tic was starting spasms on the right side of her face. "Something happened," she said.

The hospital was only a couple of blocks away, and I hit seventy miles an hour on a residential street getting there. Once there, I made one phone call, and before long the entire emergency waiting area filled with concerned friends who came to sit with me. Gretchen had been taken into a treatment room, and the situation seemed bleak—I didn't know if she was going to live or die, and I had no idea what sort of person she would be if she survived. I wondered if we would still get married and what that might be like if she didn't recover well. After a while, all the adrenaline that had fueled my mad rush to the hospital started to wear off. As I sat thinking about the question marks clouding our future, an overwhelming weight descended. I began to cry.

I was sitting between two friends, both older than me, men I respected and admired. One of them put his hand on my shoulder. I was expecting some wise, soothing words of comfort and empathy. Instead he offered this: "Get a hold of yourself. Don't do that. Don't cry. She needs you to be strong. You have to be strong."

In one way he was right. She would need a lot of strength from me, more than I ever imagined I had. But in every other way he was wrong. The best thing for me would have been to allow myself to feel what was happening. Instead, I did what he said. I pulled myself together. I stopped crying. I stopped feeling. I buried the pain.

My friend gave bad advice, but he was simply saying what he thought was the right thing to do in that moment. I'm the one who took it.

For months and years following that event, I hardly allowed myself to express any emotions. I was numb. Feelings were hard, risky, and scary. (I still struggle with allowing myself to fully feel things.) There was one emotion that occasionally erupted during those years: anger. It would flash out in unexpected ways, leaving only shame in its wake.

·✦·

Seven years later, I was in a bookstore and saw a new title from my favorite author, Frederick Buechner (pronounced *Beek-ner*). I had become aware of Buechner right after college because my minister was always quoting either him or Dietrich Bonhoeffer in sermons. I had known Bonhoeffer but not Buechner; I figured that since Buechner also had a German-sounding name, he must have been a fellow World War II martyr. I was wrong.

When I started seminary, I was assigned the Buechner book *Telling the Truth: The Gospel as Tragedy, Comedy, and Fairy Tale*. It was unlike anything I had read before—funny and wise and contemporary and timeless. I devoured that book and learned that Frederick Buechner was very much alive and at the height of his powers as a writer. I started reading every Buechner book I could find and was delighted again and again. On this particular day in the bookstore, I saw *The Clown in the Belfry* and bought it. I was immediately drawn to an essay titled "Adolescence and the Stewardship of Pain." I was working in youth ministry at the time, and the idea that Buechner had written about adolescence was intriguing. ("Stewardship," on the other hand, sounded about as exciting as mortgage amortization.) It's not an overstatement to say that essay changed my life.

Buechner invents a new etymology that suggests *adolescence* means to grow toward pain. To be an adolescent on the way to becoming an adult is to experience pain in new and significant ways. Buechner describes the difference between childhood and adolescence: "By and large children do not seem to keep score. Adolescence, as I etymologize the term, starts when scorekeeping starts."[1]

Buechner then plays with a parable Jesus tells in Matthew 25, where a man goes away and gives his servants "talents" to manage in his absence. I've heard many sermons saying this parable is about managing money, but Buechner reframes it with the unexpected suggestion that it could be about pain. The most profound part of a very profound essay says,

> What the parable is essentially about, and the question the
> parable poses is, what do we do with these mixed lives we are

given, these hands we are so unequally dealt . . . how do we get
the most out of what we are so variously and richly and hair-
raisingly given? . . . The third servant takes what he is given—
for our purposes let us focus particularly on the pain he is
given—and buries it. He takes it and hides it in a hole in the
ground and thereby, I would suggest, becomes the blood
brother and soul-mate of virtually all of us at one time or
another. . . . "I was afraid," is what the third servant says . . .
and he had good reason to be. We all of us have good reason
to be afraid. . . . So we dig the hole in the ground, in ourselves,
in our busyness or wherever else we dig it, and hide the terrible
things in it, which is another way of saying that we hide ourselves from the terrible things. . . . I think that what the parable
means is that the buried pain in particular and all the other
things we tend to bury along with pain, including joy, which
tends to get buried too when we start burying things, that the
buried life is itself darkness and wailing and gnashing of teeth
and the one who casts us into it is no one other than
ourselves.[2]

Burying pain is a way of surviving, but not a way to grow, Buechner
notes. Being alive to pain and somehow becoming a steward of it
calls us to a deeper, fuller, more honest life, out of the shallows and
into the depths: "There is no guarantee that we will find a pearl in
the depths, that the end of our pain will have a happy end, or even
any end at all, but at least we stand a chance of finding in those
depths who we most deeply and humanly are."[3]

As I read, the tears I had swallowed that night seven years earlier
came back. This was my story! How did Frederick Buechner, a writer
and pastor living hundreds of miles away in Vermont, know so much
about me?

I cried for the first time since I had "pulled myself together" that night seven years earlier. Seven years' worth of tears is a lot of tears. Frederick Buechner had used some sort of X-ray vision to gaze into my soul and see my buried secret. In that emergency waiting room, I had taken my friend's suggestion to "get a hold of myself" as an invitation to bury my pain. The numbness that followed was like being cast into outer darkness. I knew I was stuck, but I didn't know how to get out. Buechner showed me the way out, the way to becoming fully alive again.

I've told this story to several groups of people over the years, and after hearing it, people often respond by telling their stories of loss and pain. One time after I told this story, a man followed me into a men's room to tell me about the death of his daughter. I have heard heartbreaking stories of depressed and diseased spouses, sick and dying children, brain tumors, leukemia, and troubled marriages. Pain is universal, and giving ourselves permission to feel and acknowledge pain is liberating. Our stories of pain are among the most intimate gifts we can offer each other.

This is why *stewardship*—that word that didn't interest me—turns out to be such a meaningful Christian concept. To be a good steward is to ask oneself, *What am I doing with what I've been given? With my pain, yes, but more than that, with my very life? Have I shared from my deepest experiences, somehow traded with them, and improved on them? Or have I buried them, and let fear and shame and ignorance control me?*

"Something happened," Gretchen had said immediately after her stroke. But I wanted to pretend that nothing happened. It didn't work. It never works. The path to healing, to wholeness, to salvation, is always through the difficult and painful things, not around them. Buechner's words challenged me to bring my pain out and hold it to the light, a quest I have been on ever since. While such a choice is hard and risky and scary, in my experience it's the way to get your life back. Reading Buechner gave the fullness of my life back to me. Frederick Buechner changed my life.

·✦·

Buechner has excelled as a novelist, memoirist, popular theologian, and preacher. I cannot think of another writer who moves so easily from genre to genre. (Has there been another ordained minister nominated for the National Book Award or Pulitzer Prize in fiction, let alone both?) He has published for six decades. He has listened to his life with great scrutiny, because "all moments are key moments, and life itself is grace."[4]

Referring to Buechner, a wise friend once said to me, "We don't possess the man, but we do have his books," and depending on how you count, there are almost forty books to consider. Some are out of print, some seem dated, but others stand the test of time and speak as powerfully today as they did on the day they were first published. These are the essentials: books that are generative, books that expand and grow over time. I am going to explore ten "essential" Buechner books: four slim memoirs, two novels, two books of popular theology, one book about preaching, and one collection of sermons.

I write primarily for those unfamiliar with the author I consider the greatest spiritual writer of our times. I am not a literary scholar and won't pretend to offer academic analyses. Instead, I offer an invitation in a spirit of love and admiration. May we turn to these books to learn not only about "Saint Freddy of Rupert" but also to uncover what lies at the deepest places in each of us. Who knows? His words may well change your life too.

FREDERICK BUECHNER AS MEMOIRIST

I BEGIN THIS EXPLORATION of Frederick Buechner's essential books with the memoirs in order to fill in his biographical details before turning to his fiction, works of popular theology, and preaching. I'm classifying seven of Buechner's books as memoirs (although an argument can be made that there are ten), and I've identified four of the memoirs as "essentials." We'll consider them chronologically.

ESSENTIAL MEMOIRS

The Sacred Journey, 1982
Now and Then, 1983
Telling Secrets, 1991
The Eyes of the Heart: A Memoir of the Lost and Found, 1999

OTHER MEMOIRS

The Alphabet of Grace, 1970
A Crazy, Holy Grace, 2017
The Remarkable Ordinary, 2017

THE SACRED JOURNEY: THE UNIVERSAL PARTICULAR

I N 1992, FREDERICK BUECHNER and Maya Angelou appeared
together for a series of lectures sponsored by the Trinity Institute.
Buechner opened, telling about his upper-class, Ivy League
childhood that was disrupted by his father's suicide. Next the emcee
introduced Angelou, noting that she couldn't be more different from
Buechner. Not only was she an African American woman, but her
roots in abject poverty in the deep South would make her story a far
cry from the one they had just heard. As he said this, Angelou shook
her head from side to side. When she reached the microphone, she
said that he was wrong, noting, "I have exactly the same story to tell
as Frederick Buechner."[1]

Buechner was delighted, because her words affirmed one of his
core convictions, stated in the preface of *The Sacred Journey*: "The
story of any one of us is in some measure the story of us all."[2] Each
of us has a particular story—and the particular elements of Buechner's story couldn't be more different from the particular elements of
Angelou's. But what elements of each particular story are true for all

of us? Truly telling our human experiences make particular stories universal because, as the old saying puts it, what goes deepest to the heart goes widest to the world.

The power of "story" has become so ubiquitous the term is almost a cliché. But our stories are significant: stories serve as both windows to see the world through and mirrors in which we see ourselves. They function for good or for ill. "We are our stories," Rebecca Solnit writes, "stories that can be both prison and the crowbar to break open the door of that prison."[3] Stories feed what the poet Wallace Stevens called "the necessary angel" of imagination,[4] and sharing our story safely has life-giving, life-changing, and life-saving capacity.

Spiritual memoirs aren't new; perhaps the first was Augustine's *Confessions*, written some 1,600 years ago. But lately the number of story-driven spiritual memoirs has increased exponentially. Maybe they are a result of the narcissism of our age, when so many of us seem to live our lives publicly through social media. But is there more going on? The same technological advances that make it possible to live on Facebook, Twitter, and Instagram have made the world staggeringly complex. We find help navigating our way through life's challenges via the open and honest sharing of others. Great memoirs, like great novels, become equipment for living.

Spiritual memoirs feel necessary in this cultural moment, and Frederick Buechner is the godfather of today's spiritual memoir movement. He first opened the ground in 1982 with *The Sacred Journey*. The novelist Reynolds Price, writing in the *New York Times Book Review*, called the book "a beautifully successful experiment."[5] No one would call a spiritual memoir an "experiment" today. Buechner was a forerunner, and he stands as an inspirational source for many of today's practitioners of the art. The spiritual memoirist Anne Lamott calls him "America's most important living theologian" and "a brilliant, lovely religious thinker with a great sense of humor, and a first class writer."[6]

The Sacred Journey started an avalanche. It was different from autobiographies of the time—it focused on Buechner's internal spiritual development instead of external accomplishments. If Buechner had written it as a typical memoir of the time, it would have been about his development as a writer and would have culminated with the stunning success of his novel *A Long Day's Dying* in 1950, when Buechner was only twenty-three. Instead, the focus of *The Sacred Journey* is on the events that led to Buechner's embrace of Christianity (which was not predictable, since he'd grown up in a family that had no real interest in church or matters of faith) and enrollment in seminary when he was twenty-seven.

·✦·

As we explore *The Sacred Journey*, I'll include many of the particulars of Buechner's biography contained in the book while contemplating the deeper, universal truths of those particulars. I've also added some additional biographical information that helps shed light on Buechner's development.

The book's first line echoes a line used a dozen years earlier in Buechner's *The Alphabet of Grace* that suggests in essence all theology, like all fiction, is autobiographical.[7] It's a point that makes some theologians bristle because it smacks of subjectivity. (Others hear John Calvin's assertion that there is no knowledge of God without knowledge of self.)[8]

As Anne Lamott says, Buechner is a theologian, but he does not structure his thoughts or writing like a typical theologian. He does not put forth a series of propositional truths, and he deals more in doubt than certainty. What matters most is the experience of God's presence, not the objective proof of God's existence; Buechner contends in several places that presence, not proof, is the miracle we're after. This is a cornerstone of his theology. Revelation is personal: if God speaks at all, he speaks into our personal lives, and all systems of theology start first as personal experience.

Since God's Word is spoken into our lives, his Word is always an incarnate Word subject to misinterpretation and misunderstanding. This makes it a risky business to interpret the meaning of life events, to think we know what God is up to and what he might be saying to us. Yet Buechner believes there are connections that run through the seemingly random occurrences of our lives; he believes patterns emerge and meaning is suggested when we pay attention and listen to our lives. The issue isn't so much what happens but what matters. What meaning do we make of it? As Buechner lays this out in the preface of *The Sacred Journey*, he raises the question of what God might be saying through a good person's suicide, foreshadowing the key event on which this book (and in many ways his life) will turn. Although suicide references abound in Buechner's work, *The Sacred Journey* is the first of his books that plainly tells the story of that fateful day in Essex Falls, New Jersey, in November 1936, when Buechner's father sat on the running board of an automobile and breathed in the carbon monoxide that killed him. It's not a stretch to say Buechner's life and career have been a quest to understand the meaning of that event and to understand where God was when the unthinkable happened. At least one possible answer comes through in *The Sacred Journey*: although Buechner was far from God at that point in his young life, the healing that came immediately after that traumatic event was pure gift, eventually raising the thought inside Buechner that if there was a gift, then a giver was also implied. Buechner does not believe God orchestrated the event but also doesn't believe God was absent. Buechner's assertion is that somehow, even when things seem bleakest, God's grace is still an active force in our lives and world.

·✦·

Carl Frederick Buechner was born into privilege in New York City on July 11, 1926. There was wealth in the family, particularly from his paternal great-grandfather, Hermann Balthazar Scharmann, a brewer and real estate magnate. The first section of *The Sacred Journey* is titled "Once Below a Time," borrowing the phrase from Dylan Thomas, and "below time" becomes a way of describing that childhood experience of existence when time is something measured "by its content rather than its duration."[9] During this almost magical early part of his life, there is no particular narrative to be told, no events that need relaying to move the action forward. Buechner was a sensitive, bookish child, prone to spending as much time in the fantasy land of Oz as in the frequently difficult reality of his home, where his parents often argued loudly. He provides memorable descriptions of the people who filled his life, and because his family moved almost every year, it was these people rather than a house or location that constituted his true home.

The giants of his childhood were his two grandmothers. Grandmother Buechner, who lived with her husband in an apartment twelve floors above Park Avenue, was a large woman who comes off in the book as a bit of a blunt instrument as she controls the family purse strings and freely shares her opinions. Buechner's maternal grandmother, Antoinette Golay Kuhn, whom he nicknamed Naya, stands tallest in this book and in Buechner's formation. Naya is a person teeming with sophistication, imagination, and energy, a life force, and a wonderful storyteller. It is fair to surmise she was a primary source of Buechner's own great imagination: "She loved

Chesterfield cigarettes and the novels of Jean Ingelow and a daiquiri before dinner and crossword puzzles and she spoke the English language with a wit and eloquence and style that I have never heard surpassed."[10] Loosely Unitarian, it would be Naya to whom Buechner would dedicate his first novel, and Naya whom he would write into that novel as an old woman named Maroo. Naya would return as a muse throughout Buechner's writing career.

Far less light is shed on either Buechner's mother or father in *The Sacred Journey*. Writing some forty-five years after his father's suicide, Buechner's memories of his father are inconsistent. He writes that he can no longer remember what his father looked like, and when he works to bring his father back, he remembers more what others have said about him than his own recollections. He'd heard that his father was kind and gentle, a strong swimmer, and a good dancer. His father had befriended Scott and Zelda Fitzgerald when they were students at Princeton, and although he was from an elite family, he struggled to make it in business—any business—after college. His lack of success was complicated by the Great Depression, but not entirely so. He went in for foolish get-rich-quick schemes, and he also had more than economic troubles. There were big problems when his parents started drinking cocktails—and they drank a lot of cocktails. Fights and strong accusations followed (most of this is left out of *The Sacred Journey*). Buechner's father moved from job to job, and for the first fourteen years of his life, the Buechners moved often, trying to find the right place and right job for his father.

Buechner's mother, Katherine, was still alive when *The Sacred Journey* was published. He mostly leaves her out of this account of his life. She could be wonderful and difficult, and more light is shed on her and Buechner's childhood in *Telling Secrets* and *The Wizard's Tide*, published after her death. In *The Wizard's Tide* he describes navigating his childhood as "a little like piling toothpicks on top of a bottle. If you weren't very careful about the way you did it, the whole works would fall apart and go tumbling."[11] He captures the dysfunction in his family of origin plainly in *Telling Secrets*:

> If somebody had asked me as a little boy of eight or nine, say, what my secrets were, I wonder if I would have thought to list among them a father who at parties drank himself into a self I could hardly recognize as my father, and a mother who in her rage could say such wild and scathing things to him that it made the very earth shake beneath my feet when I heard them, and a two-and-a-half years younger brother who for weeks at a time would refuse to get out of bed because bed, I suspect, was the only place he knew in the whole world where he felt safe.[12]

Neither parent had religious inclinations, and Buechner and his brother, Jamie, were raised in an almost completely secular, nonreligious environment. Buechner's spiritual imagination was fed instead through books—he spent the year of 1933, when the family was living in Washington, DC, almost entirely in bed with a series of respiratory illnesses, and he writes that he lived more in the Land of Oz than the United States of America during that year.[13] He was especially enchanted by the ebullient King Rinkitink, found in the tenth Oz book, a man practically as wide across was he was tall, who appeared foolish on the surface but would be the right person to have around when things went badly. And things did go badly frequently, not only in Oz but also in the Buechner home.

One story briefly mentioned in *The Sacred Journey* and given a longer treatment in *The Wizard's Tide* illustrates the disturbing family dynamics. An eight- or nine-year-old Freddy had gone to bed when his mother came into his bedroom, handed him the family car keys, and told him not to give them to his father. A short while later, his intoxicated father appeared and begged his young son for the keys. Buechner pulled his covers up over his head and buried the clenched fist holding the keys under a pillow while his father sat on the room's other twin bed pleading for the keys. The covers and pillow sufficed that night—he didn't give his father the keys—but they couldn't protect Buechner from the pain that was coming.

·✦·

One autumn day in 1936, ten-year-old Fred and his nearly eight-year-old brother, Jamie, had woken early and excitedly because their parents were going to take them to a football game that afternoon. Fred and Jamie were passing the early morning hours playing with a roulette wheel. I assume the roulette wheel is factual instead of a literary device because what happened that morning is beyond chance and marks the moment when Buechner's "once below a time" childhood ended. Their father had looked in on the boys for a moment before going downstairs and starting the family car in the closed garage. He sat down on the running board and let the fumes kill him. Buechner's vivid memory is of hearing shouts, going to a window, and seeing his father on the ground while his grandmother and mother pumped his legs in a frantic effort to revive him.

Although the events that morning would shape and form Buechner immeasurably, what happened first in the wake of the death of Buechner's father was more grace than grief. The immediate impact of the suicide was peace. The fighting subsided with the removal of his depressed, alcoholic father. (Labels like "depressed" and "alcoholic" help explain Buechner's father's struggles, but they also diminish his humanity—*The Wizard's Tide* provides a fuller picture.) Within a few weeks the family moved halfway across the ocean to Bermuda, an Oz-like fantasy land of tropical flowers, horse-drawn carriages, and bicycles.

Grandmother Buechner, who financed the adventure, was against it, stating that the family ought to stay and face reality. Instead Buechner, his mother, and his brother escaped to a sort of garden of Eden. Although further memoirs make clear that the family's dysfunction continued following his father's suicide, the immediate impact of going to Bermuda was restorative. They may have been escaping reality, but sometimes that's what is necessary. Sometimes resolving to do it yourself prevents something gracious from being done for you. As Buechner put it, "The trouble with steeling yourself against the harshness of reality is that the same steel that secures your life against being destroyed secures your life also against being opened up and transformed by the holy power that life itself comes from."[14]

Two of the primary themes of Buechner's writing find their genesis here. The suicide of his father is the great pain that Buechner would become such a wise steward of. The journey would take decades, but the path of discovery of how one not only survives but thrives following a traumatic experience of overwhelming pain begins here. He will learn that stoicism cannot lead to a deeper place because of all it shuts out. Writing about his pain became a way to deal with it, and Buechner's writing about his pain has that universal particularity about it that has blessed countless people. Early in the summer of 2018, following the suicides of celebrities Kate Spade and Anthony Bourdain, the Centers for Disease Control and Prevention released statistics showing that American suicide rates had risen 30 percent over the past two decades. Buechner's writing is timelier than ever.

Second, Buechner's conviction that God is paradoxically at work even (or especially) through the worst that happens also starts here. The gospel, as he will come to understand it, is both tragedy and comedy. I already mentioned the question, "What is God saying through a good person's suicide?," which Buechner raises in the introduction to *The Sacred Journey*. Shortly after that, he asks, "What about sin itself as a means of grace?"[15] As he reflects (or listens), Buechner sees over and over that grace is paradoxical—what is meant for evil is used by God for good (Gen 50:20). There is joy at the deepest heart of things. And it isn't just events—Buechner sees this paradox expressed in people too. Beginning in the 1970s, the dynamic tension of characters who are simultaneously great saints and great sinners dominates Buechner's fiction, beginning with Leo Bebb and carrying through to St. Godric, St. Brendan, and the Bible's Jacob. Writing about sinner-saints carried Buechner through the most productive decades of his career. He often cites Graham Greene's whisky priest from *The Power and the Glory* as his inspiration, but I wonder if the whisky priest would speak to Buechner so tangibly, or if Buechner would have even written his greatest novels, had he not been marked by such pain from childhood.

·✦·

Bermuda was a fantasy land for Buechner, but the approach of World War II meant an evacuation of American citizens in that part of the British Commonwealth and ended the adventure. Soon Buechner was sent to boarding school at Lawrenceville, New Jersey, in the fall of 1940.

There were many father figures at Lawrenceville, among them a magnificent English teacher who helped Buechner appreciate words as things unto themselves. He saw how words carry power and energy and creative force. Worlds were opened as he read the poetry of Gerard Manley Hopkins and Shakespeare's *The Tempest*, which would become the model for Buechner's novel *The Storm* almost six decades later. When Buechner received a coveted 100 percent grade on a writing assignment, he knew he wanted to be a writer.

As an adolescent, Buechner first aspired to become a poet. Lawrenceville published its own student literary magazine called *The Lit*, and the issues from the early 1940s are filled with poems and short essays by Buechner (trying out names such as "C. F. Buechner, III" and "C. Frederick Buechner") along with James Merrill, who would become a lifelong friend and to whom Buechner would dedicate both his 1952 novel *The Seasons' Difference* and *On the Road with the Archangel* forty-five years later. Also a child of privilege (his father was the Merrill of Merrill Lynch), Jimmy Merrill would have a distinguished career as a poet and win the literary prizes—the Pulitzer and the National Book Award—that evaded Buechner.

Gazing through copies of *The Lit* today is an exercise in nostalgic irony; the pages feature advertisements with sports stars like Ben Hogan and Joe DiMaggio hawking cigarettes, alongside stylized offerings from its aspiring authors. (The faculty advisor was Gerrish Thurber, who would be a great friend for many years and to whom Buechner would dedicate his 1970 novel *The Entrance to Porlock*.) It's not unusual to find Christian references in Buechner's earliest writing; one poem from the early 1940s, for example, has a line about that pale Jew who died upon a hill and did no wrong, but Buechner downplays it, saying his motive for putting Jesus in so many of those early poems was for effect, to give the poems "some sort of aura or authority that I was afraid they lacked, to suggest that I was a much more substantial and fancier poet than I secretly believed myself to be."[16]

In the June 1942 issue Buechner published a short story called "Monkey See," in which a monkey with a razor in his hand imitates his master, who had just made a slashing motion across his throat. The monkey accidently kills himself. It is notable that this vignette, written by a then fifteen-year-old Buechner, would be included in his first novel, *A Long Day's Dying*, and be the first of several suicide references in Buechner's work. Indeed, there will be so many suicide references in Buechner's work that finding them is like spotting Alfred Hitchcock's cameo in his films—you just have to pay attention.

Buechner graduated from Lawrenceville in the spring of 1943. He moved from there to Princeton University, and his time at Princeton was interrupted by an undistinguished two-year stint in the army. During his first year at Princeton, his father's brother, Thomas Buechner, committed suicide, filling Buechner with fear that suicide was a generational curse, handed down genetically, and that he was as doomed as his father and uncle had been.

While at Princeton, Buechner experienced his first significant success as a writer, publishing a poem called "The Fat Man's Prescription" in the November 1946 issue of the prestigious *Poetry* magazine. Despite this success, his literary ambitions began to widen beyond poetry to fiction. He knew he wanted to write, but he wasn't entirely sure why or what he had to say. He took his classes more seriously than in his time before the army, and during his senior year he began working in earnest on *A Long Day's Dying*. After graduation in 1948, an appointment to join the faculty at Lawrenceville followed.

There is a gap in the memoir here, as Buechner writes little in *The Sacred Journey* about his work as an English teacher and assistant housemaster at Lawrenceville. More information comes later: a short essay titled "Fathers and Teachers" in 2008 in *The Yellow Leaves* fills in some of the gap as it relates stories of several Lawrenceville teachers who would become Buechner's colleagues and friends. *The Eyes of the Heart*, Buechner's final memoir, includes stories about the summer immediately following graduation from Princeton and before Lawrenceville, when Buechner and Jimmy Merrill lived together on Georgetown Island off the coast of Maine.

Buechner was working on his novel *A Long Day's Dying* and Merrill on his *First Poems*. No mention is made in *The Sacred Journey* about how Buechner managed to receive a contract for his first novel, and passing mention is made of a rejected marriage proposal when Buechner was twenty. Graduating from Princeton, moving to Lawrenceville—these are the headlines, but Buechner's concern is the "beyond time" moments instead, the moments in retrospect when he sees God moving him along.

A Long Day's Dying was published in January 1950 by the New York publishing house Alfred A. Knopf. (Knopf would publish Buechner's first three novels.) Dedicated "To Naya with love and wonder," the book was a startling success. The January 9 issue of *Time*, the January 16 issue of *Newsweek*, and the January 30 issue of *Life* all featured articles hailing the twenty-three-year-old as a brilliant young talent. Reading the novel today leaves me wondering about the literary tastes of 1950; it was indeed a different world. The novel is dense, written in a modernist style that focuses on the main characters' inability to connect with each other. Buechner was compared to Henry James and Marcel Proust at the time, although today he says that he'd prefer his early novels be treated as juvenilia: "I knew so little about almost anything when I wrote them. . . . More importantly I hadn't yet found my own true voice as a writer."[17]

Another gap in the memoir follows: Buechner took a one-year leave from Lawrenceville following the success of his first novel and traveled to Europe, where he had several adventures not mentioned in *The Sacred Journey.* Because his father's cousin was married to the American ambassador to Great Britain, Buechner rubbed shoulders with royalty (including Princess Margaret) and various celebrities such as Frank Sinatra and Peter Lawford. Jimmy Merrill was also in Europe, on the Spanish island of Mallorca, and Buechner journeyed to see him. He also stopped in Paris to meet the Bohemian figure Alice B. Toklas and saw Pope Pius XII conduct mass at St. Peter's in Rome on Christmas Eve. All of this is found in a chapter of *The Yellow Leaves* called "Wunderjahr," along with insight into the new novel Buechner was working on in Europe, *The Seasons' Difference.*

Few people are alive today who have followed Buechner's career since the days of *A Long Day's Dying* and *The Seasons' Difference.* Most contemporary readers discover him as a religious writer and are surprised to learn of his early literary success. What must it have felt like to have that sort of recognition and adulation at such a young age? What was it like to have Leonard Bernstein call your novel "a literary triumph" or suggest that you collaborate on an opera libretto?[18] Literature isn't gymnastics, after all, and premature publishing has its risks. Many writers don't hit their stride until they have lived four or five decades. In many ways, Buechner's career followed this arc; despite the early success, he readily admits he didn't find his voice until the Bebb books, and *Godric*, his greatest novel, was published thirty years after *A Long Day's Dying.* But the early, unanticipated success did happen, and it left its mark. In *The Sacred Journey* he writes, "From that day to this I have been driven as a writer, and to a degree as a human being too, to write something, do something, be something to justify the fluke of that early and for the most part undeserved success."[19]

The Seasons' Difference was as big a disappointment as *A Long Day's Dying* had been a success. Written in a similar modernist style, *The Seasons' Difference* is so unappreciated Buechner doesn't even refer to it by name in *The Sacred Journey.* In *The Yellow Leaves*, Buechner called it "the most unsuccessful book I have ever written and deservedly so."[20] He wonders in *The Yellow Leaves* (at the age of eighty-two) what might have happened to his career if he'd been able to produce the Bebb novels as follow up to *A Long Day's Dying*—would his star have risen the way that contemporaries and acquaintances Truman Capote's, Norman Mailer's, and Gore Vidal's did? Literary fame may have, over time, hurt each of their careers; after the brief rush of acclaim in 1950 following *A Long Day's Dying*, the distraction of great fame would not be a problem Buechner would face.

The New Yorker review called *The Seasons' Difference* "high flown nonsense."[21] *The New Yorker* had not given a particularly strong review of *A Long Day's Dying* either, saying Buechner had "a knack for spraying his scenes with either poetry or Williams Aqua Velva."[22] These words got under Buechner's skin—he would mention them in *The Alphabet of Grace* twenty years later. His "revenge" was to write a short story in a Salinger-esque *New Yorker* style, perhaps to prove that if he wanted to write like that, he could easily do it. The short story "The Tiger" (the only short story of Buechner's career) appeared in *The New Yorker* in November 1953 and would go on to win an O. Henry Award. Ironically, "The Tiger" holds up much better than Buechner's early novels, and although Buechner never anthologized it, its central image—of the man inside the Princeton mascot suit not being a real tiger—foreshadowed the "Who are they really?" questions surrounding characters such as Leo Bebb, Godric, and the Bible's Jacob.

Nothing about "The Tiger" or Buechner's frustration with *The New Yorker* is included in *The Sacred Journey*. Instead of following his literary path, the focus is more on the development of Buechner's faith, and he shares vignettes of other events in those years that moved him toward Christianity. A minister asks him to lunch, and though the minister seemed to stumble over his purpose, he asked Buechner if he'd ever considered using his talents for the sake of the church. A weekend visit to a monastery was disappointing because the monk Buechner had come to see was unavailable. Buechner also relays this story in *The Alphabet of Grace*, where he says, "This father I had come to see had gone into retreat and could see nobody—a tendency, I might add, that all my fathers seem to have had in common."[23] At the end of the weekend, the one available monk asked Buechner if he would like to make confession. Embarrassed, Buechner said yes and blurted out a few things. The monk then asked if Buechner would like to receive his blessing, and after giving the blessing, he said, "You have a long way to go."[24]

Earlier in the book, in the section on his years at Princeton, Buechner quotes a poem he'd written while in school there that ends, "I found myself, and that was everything."[25] He adds that if anyone had asked him then what or who that self was, he would have had no idea how to answer. An emptiness comes through—he knows the words of the old monk were true, he indeed had a long way to go. But he didn't know how to get there. Something was missing, but he couldn't name it. "In a world that has explained him away," he said in a sermon in the early 1960s, "God speaks to us most clearly through his silence, his absence, so that we know him best through our missing him."[26]

The universal particular is in play again: writing a bestseller at twenty-three is unique, but feeling a deep longing and awareness that there has to be something more, Someone more, is universal.

Buechner left the faculty of Lawrenceville in 1953 and moved to Manhattan to dedicate his energy to writing. The existential crisis created by his second novel's failure combined with the geographical coincidence (or was it providence?) of living in an apartment close to the Madison Avenue Presbyterian Church led Buechner to start attending. George Buttrick, the preacher, was one of the great homileticians of the mid-twentieth century.

One Sunday in 1953, Buttrick compared Jesus' refusal of a crown from Satan in the wilderness to the coronation of Queen Elizabeth, which the whole world seemingly had watched in June of that year. Buttrick noted that Jesus is a king anyway because he is crowned over and over in the hearts of believers in confession, tears, and great laughter.

Reflecting on that sermon later, Buechner wrote, "It was the phrase *great laughter* that did it. . . . It was not so much that a door opened as that I suddenly found that a door had been open all along, which I had only just then stumbled upon."[27] Sitting in church that Sunday, something happened inside the promising young novelist: "At the phrase *great laughter*, for reasons that I have never satisfactorily understood, the great wall of China crumbled and Atlantis rose up out of the sea, and on Madison Avenue, at 73rd Street, tears leapt from my eyes as though I had been struck across the face."[28] Over the years, Buechner struggled to name exactly what happened that morning in Buttrick's church. He rejects most of the typical language we hear describing religious conversion: to "become a Christian" makes it sound like an accomplishment, and "born again," in his estimation, says both too much and too little. He had been moving in the direction of Christianity for years, and on this morning he crossed a threshold. (There is good theology here: conversion is best understood as a combination of process and event.)[29]

Buechner's first awkward attempt to explain what had happened came immediately; he had dinner that afternoon with his Grandmother Buechner, who seemed bemused and pleased when he tried to articulate what had just happened to him. Feeling he needed to do something, Buechner visited Buttrick in his office a few days later to explain what had happened and ask if he should attend seminary. Buttrick at first thought seminary sounded a little extreme and offered other options for studying the faith, but eventually, perhaps recognizing the immense potential for the kingdom

of God in front of him, Buttrick took Buechner in his car and drove
north to 120th and Broadway, where Buechner enrolled in Union
Theological Seminary. The first leg of Buechner's sacred journey had
reached its culmination.

2

NOW AND THEN: FORREST GUMP'S FEATHER

T HE MOVIE *Forrest Gump* begins and ends with the image of a feather floating in the air. The feather represents Forrest's light innocence as he moves from one late-twentieth-century cultural marker to another. The feather also represents the movie's key question: Who was right? Was it Forrest's mama, who said our lives have a destiny, or Lieutenant Dan, who said we are floating around accidentally, pushed by the wind? Is there meaning in the randomness? Or are we just feathers drifting along in a series of disconnected events?

Forrest splits the difference, saying that maybe both are right, which is strong reasoning for someone with an IQ of 75. But the question—about determinism, or God's will—is one we keep asking.

Frederick Buechner believes there is much more going on. He dares to believe that God is speaking and working, even in the seemingly random and mundane parts of life (or even especially in the random and mundane parts of life). Most of the time we aren't paying attention and miss it. But God is still speaking. "The storyteller's claim," he wrote in *The Magnificent Defeat*,

> is that life has meaning—that the things that happen to people happen not just by accident like leaves being blown off a tree by

the wind but that there is order and purpose deep down behind them or inside them and that they are leading us not just anywhere but somewhere. The power of stories is that they are telling us that life adds up somehow, that life itself is like a story.[1]

As a novelist, Buechner was always looking for plot lines, and as surely as there is a plot to *Forrest Gump*, our lives have a plot as well—indeed life itself has a plot. In another *Magnificent Defeat* sermon, he said it this way: "The story of Adam is the story of each of us. We were created to serve God and each other in love, but each of us chooses instead to serve himself as God."[2] Our lives have a similar plot as the Bible: God creates, we get lost, and God works to bring us and the rest of creation back to himself.

If God is doing that, why isn't it more obvious? That question animates much of Buechner's writing, and the title of his second memoir, *Now and Then*, published one year after *The Sacred Journey*, in 1983, is an answer to that question. The title comes from the book's epigraph: "Here and there in the world and now and then in ourselves is a New Creation."[3] Buechner is quoting Paul Tillich, and he quotes a larger passage from Tillich later in the book that adds the words "mostly hidden" to the description.

Here and there, now and then, mostly hidden—these phrases are bedrock pieces of Buechner's belief about God's activity in our world. Our task is to pay attention, to stop, look, and listen for what God is doing.

·✦·

Now and Then begins where *The Sacred Journey* ended, and as with that book, the focus is not only on certain events but on how Buechner heard God speaking through those events. The book begins with Buechner's entry into seminary following his conversion and follows his life to the time of its writing. *The Sacred Journey* covered the first twenty-eight years of his life, and *Now and Then* covers the next twenty-nine.

Buechner entered Union Theological Seminary in the fall of 1954, a golden era for Union. The aforementioned Paul Tillich was on the faculty, as was the esteemed public theologian Reinhold Niebuhr, along with other prominent figures such as John Knox and Robert McAffee Brown. There was no one at Union, however, who made a deeper impression on Buechner than his Old Testament professor James Muilenburg.[4] He was so revered that on the day of his last lecture, students from the nearby Jewish theological seminary removed their shoes to indicate his classroom was holy ground. Buechner describes him memorably, saying, "He never merely taught the Old Testament, but *was* the Old Testament. . . . His faith was not a seamless garment but a ragged garment with the seams showing, the tears showing, a garment that he clutched about him like a man in a storm."[5]

Muilenburg opened the Old Testament, including the Jacob narratives in Genesis, which would deeply influence Buechner over the years and culminate in his novel *The Son of Laughter* four decades later. Muilenburg would become the character Kuykendall in Buechner's 1958 novel *The Return of Ansel Gibbs*. The character Kuykendall runs a ministry in East Harlem, which is where Buechner did field education while at Union.

The work in East Harlem was important, especially since Buechner's previous relationship with ethnic minorities had been primarily as his family's domestic help. In the 1930s Dietrich Bonhoeffer studied at Union and found much more Christian vibrancy in the nearby churches of Harlem. Union was trying to figure out ways to embrace the diversity around them, and now, on the other side of World War II, students like Buechner were doing field placements in Harlem.

Buechner's first year of study was financed by a Rockefeller grant for students who were unsure of their calling to ministry. Although captivated by his studies, Buechner still saw himself facing an either/ or choice between writing and ministry. After a year at Union, he took the next year off from school to finish *The Return of Ansel Gibbs*, a politically themed novel decidedly different in style from its predecessors. In addition to Muilenburg, Buechner would fictionalize both his parents in this book and include a version of his father's suicide. This inclusion had grave consequences, as we'll see.

The other important development during his year away from Union came when he was reintroduced to Judith Merck, a childhood acquaintance. They were married by Dr. Muilenburg in April 1956. Buechner pulls up short when he writes about Judy. Although he writes about his interior life in terrific detail, and although he writes much about his parents, grandparents, brother, and various friends, he has never written more than a line or two about Judy. In *Now and Then* he simply quotes some lovely lines from John Donne about what a miracle she was.

Why not write about Judy? It fits Buechner's pattern of not writing about loved ones while they are alive. I once asked someone who had written a bestselling memoir about how her family reacted to her book, since the author had hilariously portrayed their eccentricities. "Christmas was awful," she said. "Two of my siblings won't talk to me." Memoirists make decisions about how much to include, and often those decisions are fraught with relational peril. Buechner solves that dilemma by simply not writing about those closest to him during their lifetimes.

He does write about Judy's father, George Merck, in *Now and Then*. Merck, who died in 1957, is called "a great, tall circus of a man" and a "tycoon."[6] Merck had helmed the eponymous pharmaceutical giant Merck and Co. from 1925 to 1950 and was featured on the cover of *Time* magazine in August 1952. He owned a large amount of land around Rupert, Vermont, much of which was donated for public use as the Merck Forest and Farmland. (Buechner would later move to the Merck property in 1967.) Although Buechner doesn't write about it, clearly his marriage changed his economic position and allowed him freedom and flexibility to vocationally pursue writing over the years.

Following the year off, Buechner returned to Union for an additional two years and graduated in the spring of 1958. He was ordained that June in the Madison Avenue Presbyterian Church, with James Muilenburg preaching. The choice of denomination came for no other reason than that's where he'd been converted, listening to George Buttrick's lines about confession, tears, and great laughter. Through the years Buechner's relationship with the Presbyterian church has often been uneasy. "Just the other day," he told an interviewer in 1979, "I was invited to give a talk on 'Why I am a Presbyterian.' I told them I couldn't possibly, because I don't know why I'm a Presbyterian. . . . I keep getting letters from the Presbyterian church asking how I justify my ordination. It is a question that absolutely makes my scalp go cold. How can anybody 'justify' his ministry?"[7] His discomfort was not just about being Presbyterian—he's always been uncomfortable with the concept of ordination, often calling it the worst career move a novelist could ever make.[8] He had no answer when, at a dinner party on Long Island, his hostess asked, "I understand that you are planning to enter the ministry. . . . Is this your own idea, or have you been poorly advised?"[9]

Still, this was the path Buechner was on. Because he wasn't going into a traditional congregation, Buechner's ordination was as an evangelist, though he came to believe his primary calling was that of apologist. In September 1958, the Buechners moved to New Hampshire, where Buechner had been invited to develop a department of religion at the Phillips Exeter Academy. Soon after, he was appointed school minister at Exeter as well. It was the age of the "nego" at

Exeter, students who self-identified as negative about most every-thing, especially any form of authority—and, by extension, God, the church, and their new religion teacher. The negos came to personify what Friedrich Schleiermacher had called "religion's cultured de-spisers," and Buechner was exhilarated by the challenge.

> I had a strong suspicion that once they left Exeter, most of my captive listeners would never be caught dead in church again, and that gave me a strong sense of urgency about what I was doing. It might be the last time anybody would try to persuade them that religious faith was not as boring, banal, irrelevant, and outmoded as they thought it was, so if I didn't do it right, that would be the end of it.[10]

Late in his career he wrote that "there is an Exeter student in each of us,"[11] and it was to that inner nego that he wrote. He thought of himself as someone nonbelievers might trust: "I come so much from the same kind of world as those people who don't touch Christianity with a ten-foot pole also come from, maybe I could be a bridge, one of their own who had gone over to the other side, saying things in a language they would understand."[12]

Buechner had the negos read the apologetics of C. S. Lewis but took a different approach than Lewis. Like most apologists, Lewis presents the case for Christianity in straightforward, logical appeals to reason. The negos would read Lewis, agree with the soundness of his arguments, and still not be moved. Buechner knew there had to be more. He approached apologetics as a novelist, looking for plot lines and always leaving room for his students or readers to make their own discoveries. Along with Lewis, Buechner assigned theologians such as Karl Barth and Paul Tillich, but he felt his students needed great lit-erature to put flesh and blood on the theology, so he also assigned novels such as *The Brothers Karamazov* and *The Power and the Glory* along with plays such as *King Lear* and *Death of a Salesman*. And he assigned atheists such as Sartre and Camus, since that's who the negos were attracted to anyway. He treated both the atheists and atheistic students with respect, never attacking them straight on, leaving open the possibility they might be right, and letting the students see for themselves where the existential atheists would lead them.

· ✦ ·

Over the next five years the Buechners had three daughters: Katherine, Dinah, and Sharman. After mentioning the birth of Katherine in *Now and Then*, Buechner writes about how love, especially the love of your own children, makes you vulnerable, and his words represent the unnamed realities of Katherine's struggles at the time Buechner was writing. Eight years later, with the publication of *Telling Secrets*, he would write of a daughter's anorexia, and in other places he would mention a close family member's alcoholism, which would eventually lead him into Al-Anon. He did not write that the same person had both problems, and he always concealed the daughter's identity. However, in both new Buechner books of 2017, *A Crazy, Holy Grace* and *The Remarkable Ordinary*, Katherine, who is now a minister in the United Church of Christ, is named as the family member whose anorexia and alcoholism brought such anguish and pain.

The wisdom earned through love's pain lay in the future. Buechner spent the 1963–1964 school year on sabbatical at the Merck farm in Vermont and wrote his fourth novel, *The Final Beast*. It was his first novel since ordination, and Buechner was not prepared for the prejudicial treatment it received from the literary world because of his ordination and the book's Christian theme.

The Final Beast was born from the literature assigned at Exeter, which became standard Buechner texts that he would return to often throughout his career. At that time, he noted these books all explored the dark side of the human condition and spoke of God mostly through his absence. What he couldn't find were books that portrayed God's grace or the experience of salvation in believable ways. There was plenty of gospel as tragedy but not much gospel as comedy or fairy tale. In *The Final Beast* he attempted to write such a novel. Things happen in the novel—terrible things happen—but in the end there is grace, healing, and goodness in the sort of incomplete ways all of us are familiar with. Evil has its say, but grace gets the last word. In a 1989 interview, Buechner was asked about his intention to write about grace and mercy. Was this a moral obligation or imaginative opportunity? Buechner answered,

> Not a moral obligation—that makes it too bloodless and grim and determined! It does seem to me that there are so many books about souls being lost and so little about souls being saved. . . . So it's not with a sense of moral obligation but just a sense almost of filling this preposterous vacuum. . . . It's harder to write about salvation than it is about damnation, for one reason or another. That's my subject, the saving of souls, the presence of grace—it's a subject I love.[13]

Although he had dabbled with religious images and ideas in his previous novels, Buechner made a turn toward grace in *The Final Beast* that would continue through his career.

There is a scene in *The Final Beast*, drawn from Buechner's own experience, where the main character, a minister caught in both congregational and personal crises, prays for some word from God. Lying on his back beneath an apple tree, he cries out, "Please, please" and then adds "Jesus." Two branches strike each other.

> Just clack-clack, but praise him, he thought. Praise him. Maybe all his journeying, he thought, had been only to bring him here

to hear two branches hit each other twice like that, to see nothing cross the threshold but to see the threshold, to hear the dry clack-clack of the world's tongue at the approach of the approach perhaps of splendor.[14]

"The approach of the approach perhaps of splendor" may seem fairly innocuous, but it was a clack-clack too far for the critics. Literary ministers are typically weak, like Nathaniel Hawthorne's Arthur Dimesdale, or frauds, like Sinclair Lewis's Elmer Gantry. A struggling-yet-sincere minister who prays and gets an answer? That was too much.

"Mr. Buechner has put his foot in it," John Davenport wrote in the *Spectator*. "He writes, this formidably austere and dedicated and most delightfully amusing man, from an unfashionable centre."[15] Although Davenport's review was positive, many others were not. Worse yet, others simply ignored the book. In the eyes of the literary establishment, Buechner as the Reverend Buechner could no longer be trusted. His work was no longer literature; it was propaganda.

In his book *Culture Care*, the artist Makoto Fujimura uses the Old English word *mearcstapas*, found in *Beowulf* and translated as "border-walkers" or "border-stalkers," to describe the space that artists who affirm religious faith inhabit.[16] Buechner had no idea he was going to be pushed to the margins because of his faith, no idea that his literary fate was as a border-walker. He was stunned by the rejection: "The literary establishment by and large dropped me like a hot Presbyterian potato,"[17] and then later, beginning with the Bebb books, he felt rejection from the church world. His career has existed on the border between these two worlds, a liminal space that has made him uneasy. An example of this uneasiness is seen in his re-action, more than two decades after *The Final Beast*, to the publication of his former Exeter student John Irving's book *A Prayer for Owen Meany*, a book that also has a grace-affirming message. Irving noted his debt to Buechner in the acknowledgements and loosely based one of the main characters on Buechner. He sent Buechner a manuscript before the book was published. "I read it and loved it," Buechner said. "I told him what a really good book I thought it was and how it was, in a good sense, a very religious book. And I asked him to think what would have happened to it if it had been written by the Reverend John Irving."[18]

· ✦ ·

Buechner wrote the faith healer Agnes Sanford into *The Final Beast* as a character named Lillian Flagg. Buechner met Sanford during his years at Exeter, and though initially skeptical, he was soon convinced she was genuine. She opened Buechner to deeper understandings and experiences of prayer and the Holy Spirit. Speaking about the impact of Agnes Sanford, Buechner said,

> She was the real thing, and she had had remarkable healings. She would gather ministers together—I was one of them. She said her idea of church was Jesus standing with his arms tied behind him unable to give anybody anything, because nobody dared ask him for anything, especially the minister, for fear that if the minister prayed for the healing of old Mrs. Smith who is dying of lung cancer in the hospital and she wasn't healed, what would that do to his faith, and what will that do to the faith of the congregation? So the prayer is not prayed. [Agnes Sanford] said forget all that. Pray anyway. Pray anyway. Who knows what God can do through your prayer? That made a tremendous impression on me. So I continue. She said anybody who prays—there will be a little voice inside saying, "Oh, come on, who are you kidding?" She said that little voice inside is the product of generations of skepticism, of materialism, of not

paying attention to that kind of reality. Ignore it. Just keep doing it.[19]

Those inside the church who aren't quite sure what to make of Buechner because of his participation in the literary world would be moved by his descriptions in *Now and Then* of his new experiences in prayer after meeting Agnes Sanford: beginning the day on his knees in the Exeter school church or leading close to one thousand members of the Exeter school community in prayers of healing for two faculty members facing cancer. Prayer was a new frontier, and though he often borrowed the phrase "mostly blubbering" from James Muilenburg to describe his prayer life, Buechner's accounts of seeking God through prayer ring with sincerity and devotion. In *The Alphabet of Grace*, he used the phrase "a helpless hungerer after the marvelous"[20] to describe himself, and the world Agnes Sanford opened to him appealed deeply to his hunger for the marvelous.

In addition to prayer, Buechner brought his love of words and lively imagination to the task of preaching at Exeter. He would publish two volumes of his Exeter sermons, *The Magnificent Defeat* in 1966 and *The Hungering Dark* in 1969. Most preachers address congregations of people who have voluntarily chosen to attend church. Buechner preached to adolescent boys whose attendance at the school chapel was required. These students, led by the negos, were typically joined by a few faculty members, many of whom came out of friendship with Buechner yet held deep skepticism toward religion. Buechner found direction for the enterprise in Karl Barth's simple question posed in *The Word of God and the Word of Man*: "Is it true?"[21] Buechner believes "Is it true?" is *the* question those in church most want the preacher to address.

Buechner's nine years at Exeter produced one novel and two books of sermons. They were not as literarily productive as the years that would follow, but they were among the most fruitful of Buechner's life. His theology grew deeper and wider. His uncanny ability to connect with both skeptics and the faithful developed. He built lifelong friendships, and the addition of each daughter changed his and Judy's world. Exeter's fledgling religion department blossomed. Yet over time, teaching began to lose its challenge. He felt he had accomplished what he'd set out to do at Exeter and believed it was time for something different.

He'd spent summers and his sabbatical year at the Merck family farm in Vermont, and in 1967 Fred, Judy, and their three daughters moved there. For the second time in his life, Buechner dedicated himself to being a full-time writer. The nine years at Exeter were the longest Buechner had stayed in one place in his life. He moved to Vermont in 1967 and, with the exception of winters in Florida, never lived elsewhere.

· ✦ ·

The final section of *Now and Then*, titled "Vermont," begins in 1967 and concludes with the publication of *Godric* in 1980. Buechner was still in the midst of personal and family crises while writing this section and doesn't fully divulge what is happening around him. In some ways, there is more between the lines of this part of *Now and Then* than actually in it. However, saying that may be saying too much, because this section of *Now and Then* covers the time when Buechner fully realized his powers as a writer and began the most productive years of his writing career. There's plenty of important content here, including his well-known lines about listening to your life, words of enduring spiritual power and eloquence. On the surface, Buechner's life in Vermont sounds idyllic: living in the beauty of the Green Mountains, raising children among various horses, goats, chickens, and one enormous pig, enjoying picnics in the summer and sledding in the winter. But Buechner had moved to Vermont to write, and at first the writing didn't come easy. He grieved the loss of the Exeter community. America exploded in 1968: the Vietnam War tore the country apart, as did the assassinations of Martin Luther King Jr. and Robert Kennedy. Buechner wondered what possible use he was sitting on the side of a mountain by himself trying to write. He uses words such as "depression," "desperate," and "cheerless" to describe this time, and out of it he produced the novel *The Entrance to Porlock*, a sort of retelling of *The Wizard of Oz*. He says both that the book was born "by Caesarian section" and that "I had written myself into a blank wall."[22] It would be the last time he would be unhappy with a book because what follows is a string of significant titles. Buechner, of course, could not see any of that and described himself glumly as "a minister without a church, a teacher without students, a writer without a subject." He says the life he'd created for himself made him feel like "a rat in a trap."[23] The way out came in an invitation to give the Noble Lectures at Harvard. (He would say later, "If Harvard had invited me to come pick up gum wrappers with a pointed stick, I suppose I would have been flattered.")[24] When Buechner asked what he should speak about, the Harvard chaplain said something in the area of "religion and letters,"[25] and the word *letters* turned out to be a career-changing word. Buechner imagined letters literally, not at all in the way the chaplain had intended, but as the consonants and vowels that words are made of. "And from there I wandered somehow to the notion of the events of our lives . . . as the alphabet through which God, of his grace, spells out his words, his meaning, to us."[26] Buechner named the lectures and subsequent book *The Alphabet of Grace*. "I am a part-time novelist who happens also to be a part-time Christian because part of the time seems to be the most I can manage to live out my faith,"[27] Buechner writes in the preface of *The Alphabet of Grace*. The book focuses on one day of Buechner's life as he is writing *The Entrance to Porlock*, although he does manage to weave pieces of his life story into it. He listens to his life, and the process of writing *The Alphabet of Grace* helps him articulate what becomes his core philosophy: "Listen to your life. See it for the fathomless mystery that it is. In the boredom and pain of it no less than in the excitement and gladness: touch, taste, smell your way to the holy and hidden heart of it because in the last analysis all moments are key moments, and life itself is grace."[28]

· ✦ ·

He began writing in the library of an Episcopal church in Manchester where his youngest daughter, Sharman, was in preschool about fifteen miles from their home on Rupert Mountain. Buechner would dress in a tie every morning (to give himself the impression he was going to work), take Sharman to preschool, join the church's rector for morning prayers, and then climb the stairs to the small library and sit down to write. Some of his greatest books were written in that room during the years he made the trip to Manchester. Eventually, he would fix up a room attached to his house for writing, which he would name his "Magic Kingdom."

Lion Country, the first of the four Bebb novels, was published in 1971—twenty-one years after *A Long Day's Dying*. For the first time, Buechner felt he had fully found his voice as a writer. A *Life* magazine article he read in a barbershop about a shady minister inspired Buechner, and he used the language of grace—a gift unearned and unearnable—to describe Bebb's creation: it "was a process much less of invention than of discovery." The book was "'on the house.' It floated up out of my dreaming."[29] Previous novels had taken a year or two to write; the first Bebb book was finished in less than three months.

With Leo Bebb, Buechner took the tie off, so to speak, and let his sense of humor out to play. As in *The Final Beast*, there is tragedy in the Bebb books, but the gospel is more comedy and fairy tale than tragedy here. (His earliest novels, by comparison, were humorless.) Bebb is both Buechner's alter ego and antithesis—a plump Southerner who lives vibrantly as he hands out questionable diplomas and has a criminal record for indecent exposure. When Buechner first imagined Bebb, he saw him as a villain, but as he wrote, Bebb became a kind of saint, the first of a string of deeply flawed saints that dominate Buechner's fiction. Bebb also is a later incarnation of King Rinkitink of the Oz books and Tristam Bone from *A Long Day's Dying*.

But the Bebb books are a long way from *A Long Day's Dying*. They aren't set, as Buechner's first books were, in the patrician world of East Coast society; they take place in seedy places like the Salamander Motel in Armadillo, Florida. The pretense and labored style of Buechner's first books is long gone too; Leo Bebb would never stand for it. Bebb brought depths of self-expression out of Buechner. Buechner let salty language fly, he cracked jokes, and let himself be fully himself on the page. Bebb led Buechner to expose himself—not indecently, but, as he says in *Now and Then*, without Bebb he never could have written either *The Sacred Journey* or *Now and Then*. Leo Bebb changed Frederick Buechner's life, but it is clear in the way Buechner writes about the discovery of Bebb that this wasn't just Forrest Gump's feather blowing in the wind. The gifts had come from a Giver.

That's not to say there are especially clear or deep nuggets of wisdom in the Bebb books. Many Christian readers have been put off by them. But they are pure Buechner—full of paradox and ambiguity, with a sense of God's grace always lurking just below the surface for those with open eyes and ears ready to see and hear.

·✦·

Before ending *Now and Then* with an account of the publication
of *Godric*, Buechner writes about taking Katherine and Dinah to
boarding school (at the Groton School in Massachusetts, where
Katherine was in the first group of women to graduate). He revisits
the idea of how having and loving children opens a parent up to the
vulnerabilities of love. When he says things like, "The world does
cruel and hurtful things"[30] and mentions the acuteness of his suffering when his children suffered, these are veiled references to Katherine's struggles. He was still reeling when *Now and Then* was written,
and the decade of the 1980s would see Buechner find significant
healing through participation in twelve-step groups for family
members of alcoholics and his own work with different therapists.

Godric, published in 1980, is Buechner's greatest accomplishment
as a novelist, and he finishes *Now and Then* with a few stories about
its creation and quoting some of its most memorable lines. For all
this, he is probably still too close to *Godric's* writing at the time to
fully know what the book would come to mean to him.

Later editions of *Now and Then* contain the subtitle *A Memoir of
Vocation*, and the book does cover career moves like Buechner's prep-
aration for ministry at Union, his years as a school minister at Exeter,
and leaving to become a full-time writer in Vermont. Yet as with *The
Sacred Journey*, it's more than a description of places and events.
Buechner pays close attention—he listens to his life—and as he looks
back on the people and places of his life, he doesn't see himself as a
feather blown by the wind but sees God's hand in it all, moving him
forward. Ultimately, *Now and Then* is about the education and matu-
ration of a person with a marvelous facility for language putting his
gifts to work for the kingdom of God.

On that fall day in 1953 when Buechner asked George Buttrick
whether he should attend seminary, Buttrick said it would be a shame
to lose a good novelist for a mediocre preacher. He needn't have worried.

TELLING SECRETS:
A DEEPER HONESTY

I N THE EIGHT YEARS following the publication of *Now and Then*,
three experiences shaped Frederick Buechner in significant ways.
First, Buechner's mother, Katherine, died in 1988, giving him new
freedom to fully tell the story of his childhood. Second, he had continued to work with a therapist and gained new insight into his
family of origin. Third, he had joined Al-Anon, which, like therapy,
shed new light on the rules he'd lived by growing up. The result is
Telling Secrets, a little stick of dynamite and the most revealing and
emotionally gripping of his memoirs.

In *Telling Secrets*, Buechner jumps in quickly, grabs the reader by
the collar, and doesn't let go. "One November morning in 1936 when
I was ten years old," he writes, "my father got up early, put on a pair
of gray slacks and a maroon sweater, opened the door to look in
briefly on my younger brother and me, who were playing a game in
our room, and then went down into the garage where he turned on
the engine of the family Chevy and sat down on the running board
to wait for the exhaust to kill him."[1]

First sentences make promises, and the promise that begins *Telling
Secrets* is, appropriately enough, that secrets will be divulged—in this

case secrets about his father's death. I have read *Telling Secrets* at least a dozen times, and every time I have to put it down after about five pages and take a deep breath. I return to it over and over because I find its honesty and insight irresistible. The first secret told is not the suicide—Buechner had done that in *The Sacred Journey*—but how his family responded (or didn't even seem to respond) to the suicide. The fact that his father had existed at all became their secret. They didn't talk about him, and they certainly didn't talk about the manner of his death. There was no funeral, no acknowledgment that he had lived but wasn't alive anymore, no acknowledgement that they were grieving. He was seemingly forgotten, and everything about him was buried and sent underground.

"Don't talk; don't trust; don't feel": these were the rules his family operated by, rules he would have gained insight into from his group for adult children of alcoholics. Buechner's participation in Al-Anon had opened his eyes anew not only to his childhood but also to some of his experiences as an adult. Buechner reveals what had happened to him in 1958, when he had published a fictionalized account of his father's suicide in *The Return of Ansel Gibbs*. The word he uses to capture his mother's response to that book is *fury*.[2] Buechner was thirty-two when *Ansel Gibbs* was published but felt as shamed, humiliated, and horrified as a ten-year-old boy. What had he done? He felt sure he had broken some sort of sacred trust. He did not assert his right to share that story; instead he felt guilt and a grim sense that he'd made a horrible mistake. In a 1992 interview he put it this way: "It is a mark of dysfunctional families that they never tell their secrets, and my mother presided over that dictum like Victoria over the British Empire."[3]

Over two decades after the publication of *Ansel Gibbs*, when Buechner was in his fifties and his mother was in her eighties,

Buechner summoned the courage to directly mention his father's suicide in *The Sacred Journey*. At this point, he writes, he felt he could tell the story because he was sure his mother didn't read what he wrote anymore for fear of what she'd find there.[4] The pain Buechner feels is evident: imagine how it might feel to be a celebrated author who had been nominated for the National Book Award and Pulitzer Prize yet also be certain your mother won't read your work.

His mother, almost entirely absent from *The Sacred Journey* and *Now and Then*, is the focus of the early pages of *Telling Secrets*. She was a beautiful woman, but her beauty, in Buechner's estimation, kept her from fully growing as a human being. She didn't have to do anything to merit the love or attention she received, and never developed much compassion or generosity of spirit. Two failed marriages followed her marriage to Buechner's father, and she spent the final years of her life alone in a world that got smaller and smaller as she aged. Buechner's critique is devastating. Buechner loved his mother, but she was also a source of anguish and frustration. Above all he sensed that his mother never had the courage to face life head-on. As a result, she never fully became the person she might have become.

Over the years her hearing failed, and she had a habit of closing her eyes when speaking, which made communication a special challenge. Buechner felt she used her hearing loss and closed eyes as tools to keep the world and its pain at arm's length.

Just as quickly as Buechner moves in the initial pages from his father's suicide to the portrait of his mother, he shifts again to tell another secret: his startling discovery that so many of her problematic coping behaviors lived on in him. There was trouble in his own house that he had turned a deaf ear and blind eye to. In the late 1970s his daughter Katherine had graduated from the Groton School, entered Princeton, gotten married, and then dropped out of school.

She had become both an alcoholic and anorexic. She wound up
hospitalized in Seattle, where a court-ordered feeding tube saved her
life. Her problems were complex, but Buechner saw himself as an
integral part of them: "I didn't have either the wisdom or power to
make her well. . . . Everything I could think to do or say only
stiffened her resolve to be free from, among other things, me."[5] He
describes himself as "haggard, dithering, lovesick,"[6] and as someone
who bounced into heaven if she ate a piece of toast or descended to
hell if she skipped dinner.

Katherine's illness happened before the writing of *The Sacred
Journey* and *Now and Then*, but there were only hints of her struggle
in those books. (As we will explore in detail later, Buechner's novel
Godric was born out of the crucible of this experience.) Even in
Telling Secrets Buechner holds back—he doesn't use Katherine's name
or tell much of her story. He says both that it wasn't his story to tell
and that he didn't fully understand her story because he didn't fully
know what it felt like to be her. Instead, he focuses on his part in the
story: on how he felt complicit in her illness and on how often ministers especially don't take care of themselves. He mentions how easy
it is to write words like this but so hard to live them. Yet when he
and his wife, Judy, visited Katherine in the hospital in Seattle, he felt
an overwhelming peace and awareness of God's presence. As
Buechner watched his daughter recover, he had a clear sense that
things were not well inside him and that he also needed healing.

·✦·

Instead of exploring the ways he wasn't well in more depth,
Buechner makes a turn here into theology. He fleshes out his understanding of the tensions between human freedom and God's sovereignty. These are questions that have occupied philosophers and

theologians for centuries, and in many ways both *The Sacred Journey* and *Now and Then* are animated by this tension. (It's Forrest Gump's feather again.)[7] Are humans making free choices, or is God directing the action? What, precisely, does Buechner mean when he keeps returning to the idea of God speaking through the events of our lives? How do we reconcile the concept of a loving God with the reality of tragedy? He had asked what God might be saying through a good man's suicide in the first pages of *The Sacred Journey*, and more than his daughter's illness, it is his father's suicide he is thinking of here. Was this God's will? How does Buechner understand the relationship between human freedom and God's sovereignty?

Lest this seem too much like an esoteric exercise, Buechner brings it to life in the novel *Brendan*, which was written during this period. St. Brendan, known as Brendan the Navigator, does precious little navigation on his first voyage. He sails in a leather curragh, a small Irish boat, without a rudder; he leaves it to the wind, or God, to decide his fate.

Which is it? In *Telling Secrets*, Buechner suggests and rejects different analogies. He rejects God as chess player, moving us like pieces on a board, as well as God as puppeteer, pulling the strings of every human action. Along with these analogies, he also rejects the idea that his father's suicide was God's will. Buechner believes his father alone willed his suicide. A third analogy is suggested: God as the great director, giving cues from the wings. As he says this, he asserts that God was somehow still mysteriously present that day when Buechner's father took his own life.

His reasoning strikes a chord in me. It is hard to imagine a loving God directly willing cataclysmic disaster or personal tragedy. It is especially unconscionable to say, as many have done, that tragic events are God's direct punishment for sin. (Jesus rejected this sort of cruel reasoning with his comments about the Tower of Siloam in Luke 13.)

Many conceive of human freedom and divine sovereignty as opposite seats on a giant seesaw—the greater human freedom, the less of God's sovereignty; the greater God's sovereignty, the less human freedom. There are dangers when either end is all the way up. When human freedom is the high end, one begins to bump into deism, where God created the world but now stands aside—or some forms of process theology, where God is as surprised as anyone by the unfolding of history. Such a God seems like no God at all. But when divine sovereignty is at the top, we get a God causing humans to sin and being responsible for every tragedy. (It's tragedy that we struggle with—as everyone knows who has ever whispered, "Thank you, Jesus," when a parking spot opens or who has looked heavenward after a walk-off home run, we have no trouble attributing the good things in life to God.)

Thinkers have devised all sorts of strategies to get away from this zero-sum game. Instead of points on a line, some imagine human freedom and divine sovereignty as concentric circles, with human freedom nestled inside divine sovereignty. The British musician-theologian Jeremy Begbie uses the illustration of a musical chord: one note playing full force doesn't mean another note can't also be playing full force.[8] That brings up echoes of the idea of "secondary causality," used by thinkers like Thomas Aquinas. Human freedom exists because God has made it possible: God's agency enables human agency rather than existing in competition with it. When humans move toward God, God is directly acting on them, making it happen at the same time humans are exercising their agency. But when human beings deviate from their created purpose, God isn't the one causing it. Still others have been helped by Leslie Weatherhead's book *The Will of God*, which delineates a difference between God's intentional will, permissive will, and ultimate will.[9] Others use similar language, making a distinction between God's active will and permissive will and separating what God directly causes to happen from what God allows to happen.

This is important because it affects how we conceive of key aspects of the Christian life. For example, why employ intercessory prayer if God either has his hands tied or if he's already orchestrated everything? And this is fundamental to the tensions surrounding the human role in salvation, played out centuries ago by Augustine and Pelagius and still today between Calvinists and Arminians.

This is also important for understanding Buechner. While he insists again and again that life has a plot and that God is active in our most mundane moments, in *Telling Secrets* he seems to elevate human freedom over divine sovereignty, writing that "events happen under their own steam as random as rain."[10] In an otherwise positive article about Buechner in *Christianity Today*, Russell Moore writes, "Buechner's articulation of free will makes me wonder how God could be authoring a plot for the universe (or for me) without a stouter sense of sovereignty."[11] Moore may well have this very line from *Telling Secrets* in mind.

Moore believes Buechner comes up short here. Yet if we conceive of a post-fall universe where God allows human freedom, we must acknowledge freedom brought sin, sin brings chaos, and chaos is by definition as random as rain. On top of that, remember that Buechner always ventures into theology with a pastor's heart. The best pastoral answer in the face of inexplicable tragedy isn't an answer at all. It is presence, a notion Buechner returns to repeatedly. This side of eternity, we won't ever get all the answers. There could not possibly be a satisfactory answer to the puzzle of Buechner's father's suicide. What matters most is that even in that incredibly dark moment, God did not abandon Buechner's father. This is a pastoral word, because what we all desire more than answers is God.

Buechner relates one such holy experience of God's presence in *Telling Secrets*. During the dark days of his daughter's anorexia, he stopped his car by the side of a road, lost in painful thoughts. A car approached with a personalized license plate spelling out T-R-U-S-T. Buechner recognizes this might just be the sort of joke life plays on us once in a while, but he affirms it as something else. He sees it as a word from God. It was "the one word out of all the words in the dictionary that I needed most to see exactly then."[12]

·✦·

Buechner had two very different teaching experiences in the years between *Now and Then* and *Telling Secrets*. Both experiences are filled with theology and come as a surprise to those who place Buechner on the left side of the theological spectrum.

In the winter of 1982, he accepted an invitation to teach preaching at Harvard Divinity School. He went with fond memories of the community he'd been a part of at Union Theological Seminary in the 1950s and high expectations simply because this was Harvard. He was in for a series of unpleasant discoveries.

Buechner unwittingly caused a stir when he prayed before his first class, which his professors at Union had regularly done. He did not know this sort of display was out of fashion at Harvard, and he would soon come to realize he was far away from many of his students, some of whom were humanist atheists. He couldn't fathom why atheists were in divinity school: "To attend a divinity school when you did not believe in divinity involved a peculiarly depressing form of bankruptcy."[13] Nor could he understand what an atheist might preach about. Students objected to his assigned texts—Shakespeare and

G. K. Chesterton were judged to be sexist, and Graham Greene's *The Power and the Glory* was called racist. While Buechner did not necessarily disagree with all of those judgments, he felt that "if your principles keep you from being able to draw on the wisdom of writers of earlier generations who didn't happen to share those principles or even to be aware of them, you may keep your principles intact but at the same time do yourself a tragic disservice."[14]

Buechner's sense was that the pluralism the school was so proud of had devolved into factionalism, "and that if factions grind their separate axes too vociferously, something mutual, precious, and human is in danger of being drowned out and lost."[15] Buechner, always an open thinker, had run into students he struggled to connect with. In a fit of exasperation after sharing deeply from his life, he told his class that "they reminded me of a lot of dead fish lying on cracked ice in a fish store window with their round blank eyes."[16] He felt they were unable to articulate what they believed at a deep level, and his own convictions about preaching became clearer. His students were interested in preaching about ideas. Buechner saw the task as not being about ideas but about Jesus, "a Mystery before which, before whom, even our most exalted ideas turn to straw . . . new ideas about peace and honesty and social responsibility may come, but they are the fruits of the preaching, not the roots of it."[17] There are echoes here of a sermon he preached years earlier at Exeter:

> If I thought that when you strip it right down to the bone, this whole religion business is really just an affirmation of the human spirit, an affirmation of moral values, an affirmation of Jesus of Nazareth as the Great Exemplar of all time and no more, then like Pilate I would wash my hands of it. The human spirit just does not impress me that much, I am afraid.[18]

·✦·

A second teaching experience came at Wheaton College in Illinois, a school many literal and figurative miles away from Harvard Divinity School. Before going there to teach, Buechner had already donated his papers to Wheaton for two primary reasons. First, they had asked. Second, the school already had papers from the likes of C. S. Lewis, G. K. Chesterton, Dorothy Sayers, George MacDonald, and J. R. R. Tolkien, and Buechner was delighted with the company his papers would keep. In the fall of 1985, he accepted an invitation to teach a literature class at Wheaton.

Still, Buechner headed to Wheaton with reservations. He knew it was Billy Graham's alma mater, and Buechner had never had much experience in the evangelical world a figure like Billy Graham personified. On top of that, there was the famous Wheaton Pledge, with its moral restrictions and requirements that Buechner felt sent the wrong message about what lies at the heart of Christianity.

He had decided to assign *The Brothers Karamazov* in his literature class, and he wondered whether this would upset the school's administration because of the withering attack Ivan Karamazov makes on the idea of a loving God. Buechner was surprised to learn *The Brothers Karamazov* was a standard text in the English department, and he decided that whatever the term *evangelical* meant, it did not mean closed-minded.[19] The seriousness with which the Wheaton community applied the Christian faith to the task of education moved Buechner. The great eastern universities he was familiar with had, by comparison, long abandoned the faith they were founded on.

Once, when Buechner was having lunch with two students, one asked the other what God was doing in his life. Buechner didn't have a category for a question like that and couldn't conceive of anyone he knew on the East Coast ever asking it. The question moved

Buechner: "If there is anything in this world I believe, it is that God is indeed doing all kinds of things in the lives of all of us."[20]

At Wheaton, Buechner found people who not only believed as he did but weren't embarrassed about expressing it. It was "like finding something which, only when I tasted it, I realized I had been starving for for years."[21]

•✦•

There are three section titles to *Telling Secrets*. The first, "The Dwarves in the Stable," is a reference to *The Last Battle*, C. S. Lewis's final Narnia book. The second, "The White Tower," refers to a part of the Tower of London that held a dungeon called "Little Ease." The third section is "The Basement Room," a reference to the type of room where Al-Anon groups usually meet. The unconditional acceptance, lack of hierarchy, honesty, lack of pretension, and devotion to God (albeit as "Higher Power") in Al-Anon provide Buechner with a model of what the church is intended to be instead of the dysfunctional family many churches are. It didn't hurt Buechner's estimation of the groups when he learned that they typically began with the serenity prayer written by Reinhold Niebuhr, his old seminary professor. Buechner's daughter Katherine participated in Alcoholics Anonymous as part of her recovery and suggested to her father he might be helped through participation in a twelve-step group. "You can't help thinking," he writes in *Whistling in the Dark*, "that something like this is what the Church is meant to be and maybe once was before it got to be Big Business. Sinners Anonymous."[22]

One place the impact of Al-Anon comes out is in the novel *Brendan*, published in 1987. Brendan was an Irish saint who lived in the sixth century and may have sailed as far as Newfoundland and Florida in search of Tir-na-n-Og, a paradise thought to exist beyond the horizon.

As with *Godric*, Buechner imagines a life for Brendan that fills in details from a fairly bare-boned historical record. *Brendan* is an interesting novel, but it never quite reaches the heights *Godric* reached. The novel wasn't born out of the same internal anguish that *Godric* was—Buechner was a healthier person when *Brendan* was written. However, there is a scene in *Brendan* that rings with the unconditional acceptance of groups like Al-Anon. Brendan and his friend Finn meet Gildas, a Welsh monk-historian. When Gildas stands, they realize that he is missing a leg. As he attempts to get his walking stick, he loses his balance and is headed for the ground when Brendan catches him.

"I'm as crippled as the dark world," Gildas said.

"If it comes to that, which one of us isn't, my dear?" Brendan said.

After a few moments of silence, the scene ends: "To lend each other a hand when we're falling," Brendan said. "Perhaps that's the only work that matters in the end."[23]

That line could be used as a slogan for twelve-step groups. What Buechner loved most about Al-Anon was the sense that all they had was God and each other:

> One of the luckiest things I ever did, to use one kind of language—one of God's most precious gifts to me, to use another—was to discover that I was one of them and that there were countless others like me who were there when I needed them and by whom I also was needed. I have found more spiritual nourishment and strength and understanding among them than I have found anywhere else for a long time.[24]

·✦·

One way to understand memoirs is as exodus stories: there is bondage, release, entry into a new land, and discovery of a new covenant. At one point in *Telling Secrets*, Buechner refers to suicide as his father's exodus, of the covenant he made with his mother and brother never to talk about him, and of their sojourn following it in Bermuda as a kind of promised land.

Telling Secrets can be seen as Buechner's new exodus story. He begins with his father's suicide and reflections about his mother as introduction to his daughter's anorexia. His realization is that in its own way, his family with his wife and children are in bondage, they have dysfunctions that echo his family of origin and are made manifest in Katherine's anorexia. The deliverance that happens comes in stages—Katherine's stay in the hospital in Seattle and slow recovery, her participation in a twelve-step group and recommendation that Buechner do the same, and his work in therapy and Al-Anon all are a part of the movement out of bondage to a different way of being. The new covenant is the new rules he learns to live by. The promised land isn't a different geographical location; it's more like the home Dorothy longed for in Oz or the one the prodigal son remembered when he was in a distant country. Is it any wonder that a few years after *Telling Secrets*, Buechner published a book with many memoir-ish elements called *The Longing for Home*? In that book he acknowledges that three of his most significant novels—*Godric*, *Brendan*, and *The Son of Laughter*—all have elements of the search for home in them. His conclusion in *The Longing for Home* is that "the home we long for and belong to is finally where Christ is. I believe that home is Christ's kingdom, which exists both within us and among us as we wend our prodigal ways through the world in search of it."[25]

·✦·

At the close of *Telling Secrets*, Buechner relays a significant experience during a therapy session that is part of coming home, which also helped him heal many painful memories. His therapist suggested he write with his nondominant hand, which caused him to slow down and write more as a child than an adult. Then she suggested he imagine a conversation with his father. What did Buechner want to say to him? What would he say to his son? It is a memorable conversation. Toward the end of their conversation, his father tells him the great secret he didn't know then but knows now: there is nothing to worry about.

"What do you know, Daddy? . . . my dearest Dad and father?"

"I know plenty, and it's all good. I will see you again. Be happy, for me."[26]

Buechner is writing a new ending for their relationship. Instead of it ending with all the unanswered questions that follow a suicide, it now ends with the father telling the son he loves him and is proud of him, and that everything is going to be alright.

About the same time, Buechner had a dream about his mother. In the dream, he and his brother Jamie see her in her apartment, preparing to go out to meet someone. She is full of energy as she gets ready to see someone she disliked for over sixty years, leading Buechner to conclude the kingdom of heaven had to be where she was and is. The dream signified that his mother was "back in business,"[27] and the dysfunctional rules she had laid down—like the rule that her sons had no right to be happy if she was unhappy—no longer applied. Throughout *Telling Secrets*, Buechner is not only making peace with his parents but honoring his father and mother by honoring the good within them and forgiving the pain they caused him.

In this way, the end of *Telling Secrets* foreshadows the next memoir, *The Eyes of the Heart*, where Buechner will bring his grandmother Naya back to life and explore the events of his life while also thinking deeply about his death. It also leaves the reader with an image of

Buechner as someone who has grown emotionally and spiritually, as someone who has gone "further up and further in," to borrow C. S. Lewis's phrase. Buechner was sixty-five when *Telling Secrets* was published, and the book demonstrates the maturity and gravitas of not only an author at the height of his literary powers but a Christian not content to stay in the shallows, who embraces the pain and complexity of life and finds wonder and mystery and God's grace in it.

THE EYES OF THE HEART:
REMEMBERING THE LOST
AND FOUND

IBRING NAYA INTO THE MAGIC KINGDOM."[1] *The Eyes of the Heart* begins with a reference to Frederick Buechner's maternal grandmother, Naya. But this time he isn't remembering Naya. Instead, Naya (who died in 1961) is there with him.

This beginning signals that *The Eyes of the Heart* is going to be a different kind of memoir, especially when set next to Buechner's previous three. The layout is different—the others begin with a short introduction, have three sections (with titles related to their content), and are each just over a hundred pages long. *The Eyes of the Heart* has no introduction, has eight untitled chapters, and is almost two-hundred pages long.

The book is also different because there is no chronological story to tell. It's been eight years since *Telling Secrets*, and Buechner has spent those years doing the same things he'd done since moving to Vermont in 1967. There are no milestone achievements to report. What's new is actually what (or who) is gone. Buechner has experienced significant loss—his oldest friend, Jimmy Merrill, died in 1995, and his brother, Jamie, died while Buechner was writing this book. Losing a friend of five decades and a brother (as well as entering his seventies) brings Buechner's own mortality into focus, and the approach of his death casts a shadow here: "It is not my ultimate destination that preoccupies me at this point so much as it is the nature of the departure."[2] *The Eyes of the Heart* is a book about death and what happens after we die.

The other central theme of the book is the "Magic Kingdom." The Magic Kingdom is Buechner's three-room "haven and sanctuary"[3] at his Vermont home. The name started as a joke—playing on Disneyland—but like many names first suggested in jest, it stuck. Buechner's original title for the book was *The Magic Kingdom*, but his publisher, not wishing to tangle with the Disney empire, turned that down. Buechner's Magic Kingdom consists of an entryway, where he keeps his voluminous collection of family archives, the office where he writes, and his library. The library *is* magic, at least to those who share Buechner's literary inclinations. He says he expects visitors to quake because of the treasures therein, and Buechner has an amazing collection. His childhood books are there: his Uncle Wiggily and Oz books, and volumes of *Alice in Wonderland* and *Alice Through the Looking Glass* signed by the original Alice when she visited this country as an old woman in 1932. There are early and original editions of authors like Charles Dickens, John Donne, Ben Johnson, and Herman Melville. Over the years Buechner has collected autographs of literary heroes like Anthony Trollope, Mark Twain, and Henry James, alongside the signature of Queen Elizabeth I. There is a bust of his friend Jimmy Merrill too. There is also a heart-shaped rock Buechner found on the island of Outer Farne, where Godric had a vision of St. Cuthbert. In Buechner's telling, Cuthbert says that when you leave home, you leave a bit of your heart behind, but when you visit a place, you send a bit of your heart ahead. Buechner visited this uninhabited North Sea island to pay tribute to Godric, saw a rock lodged in a crack when he landed, and discovered it was heart-shaped after prying it loose with a pocket knife. It gave him the distinct impression that he'd been expected, and he saved the rock as a holy relic.

The Eyes of the Heart unfolds as an interplay between people that have been lost and objects that have been collected. There is a valedictory feel to the book—one wonders if perhaps Buechner was thinking this might be his final book. *The Sacred Journey* and *Now and Then* are about a young man on his way somewhere; *Telling Secrets* contains the reflections of a middle-aged man looking deeper into himself; and *The Eyes of the Heart* is an old man looking back at his life, especially thinking of those he's loved and lost. There is a sadness over everything, but there is also peace, integrity, and beauty.

·✦·

What happens after we die? Although I recently saw a headline about the increasing signs that human consciousness remains after death,[4] and doctors don't quite know what to make of the reports from revived people who talk about seeing their body from above or moving toward a warm light, life after death truly is "eyes of the heart" territory. Wouldn't we all like to talk about it with a loved one who has already passed on? Buechner puts his questions directly to Naya, and as you read, you lean in for her answers, forgetting momentarily that she's not really there at all.

Or maybe she is really there. It feels like she is. As she talks, it's apparent she isn't in heaven, at least the heaven that most Christians imagine. Perhaps this is purgatory, although Buechner doesn't use that word, or a parallel universe, or simply the space we occupy between death and the final resurrection. Concerning death, Naya says that it isn't the person who passes away but the world that passes away from the person. The world slows down enough to step off: "It was rather like getting off a streetcar before it has quite come to a stop," she says, "a little jolt when my foot first struck the pavement, and then the world clanged its bell and went rattling off down the tracks without me."[5]

Is that what death is, a moment when the world moves away in a different direction? Buechner's mother, who avoided speaking about death or even saying the names of those she'd loved who had died, surprised him one day by asking if he really believed "anything *happens* after you die?"[6] Because of her hearing loss, Buechner tried shouting his affirmative answer, but some things are not suited for shouting. As he spoke in a normal voice, he could see that she not only wasn't hearing but also wasn't listening as well. He wound up writing his response, which becomes a sort of apologia for life after death. He lists three reasons: (1) He couldn't imagine God going to the trouble of creating our world and then assigning that creation to oblivion. (2) If all the good and evil people simply wound up with the same fate in the grave, life is nothing more than a dark comedy. Life has never felt that way to him—instead it feels very much like a mystery. (3) Because Jesus said it was so.[7]

When he later asked his mother about the letter, she said it had made her cry. Buechner's suspicion is it wasn't the letter's contents that made her cry but the nearness of her own death; he supposed that she'd asked about death in the first place because she knew her own death wasn't far off. Over the years, their relationship worked as long as things were kept on a surface level, but if Buechner tried to go deeper, it got complicated. Here he tells about the last time they saw each other. She had been complaining about one of the women who helped care for her, and when Buechner defended the woman, his mother asked, "Why do you hate me?" Later, before he left, she said, "You have always been my hero." Those two sentences— "Why do you hate me?" and "You have always been my hero"—were the last words she said to him face to face.[8] Although her death gave him the freedom to write about the many ups and downs of their relationship in *Telling Secrets*, and although by the time of *The Eyes of the Heart* it had been more than a decade since she'd died, it's obvious they still aren't done with each other. He thinks about bringing her back the way he's brought Naya back, but he decides against it for fear that she might be too much for him.

Buechner is not done with his father either. He contemplates bringing his father back but decides against it, fearing in this case that his father may be not enough for him. Thinking about the father void he's lived with most of his life produces a remarkable sentence: "I suppose one way to read my whole life—my religious faith, the books I have written, the friends I have made—is as a search for him."[9] It has been sixty-three years since his father's suicide, and the hole is still there: "I doubt that a week has gone by without my thinking of him. In recent years I doubt that a single day has gone by. Who on earth was he?"[10] In the family archives he has pictures of his parents before their marriage. His father had been the captain of the water polo team at Princeton, and his mother was a great beauty; they eloped together in the summer of 1922. "I asked a woman who had known them back then what they had been like," he writes. "I thought she might be able to tell me something she had glimpsed in them, some fatal foreshadowing. . . . Without a moment's hesitation the woman I had questioned said simply, 'I wanted to be just like them.'"[11] Looking at a photograph taken the day before their elopement, he thinks about being able to go back to warn them against doing it, but then wonders, "How I can wish undone this thing they are on the threshold of doing without wishing myself undone?" Even though it will cost his father his life at the age of thirty-eight, and even though his mother will carry a burden of "guilt and regret and self-condemnation" to the grave, he "would not have missed the shot at the world their misalliance gave" him.[12] As in the previous memoirs, we are moving into "Forrest Gump's feather" territory.

As he looks at the picture of his parents, he notices three women sitting behind them, two middle-aged and one elderly. He proposes that they are the three fates from Greek mythology, and the elderly woman is Atropos, the oldest of the fates who would cut the threads and end the lives of mortals. "Her right hand," Buechner writes, "is concealed behind my father's shoulders and in it the fatal shears."[13] Buechner opens the door again to his belief that our lives are not cosmic accidents but stories that have meaning, even if that story will result in tragedy. No matter how we got here, we are here, and it is not an accident. The task for Buechner, as it is in some sense for all of us, is to make peace with the past and with those who have loved us imperfectly and those we've loved imperfectly by forgiving and asking for forgiveness.

· ✦ ·

Among the losses Buechner reflects on in *The Eyes of the Heart* is that of Jimmy Merrill. Buechner sees his friend's image daily—the bust of Merrill on a shelf in the Magic Kingdom was created by the sculptor Morris Levine in 1948, when Buechner and Merrill spent a summer together in Maine writing their first books. Friends for fifty-five years, Buechner and Merrill met at Lawrenceville. Merrill was "fat, effeminate, bespectacled, with braces on his teeth, and nicknamed

Toots."[14] His only defense was his wit until he found a friend in
Buechner. They took to calling themselves the "Uglies," a term
Buechner would insert into his second novel, *The Seasons' Difference.*
"An Ugly," Buechner writes, "was bookish, introspective, completely
nonathletic and tended to feel awkward and helpless and lost, especially on occasions when the rest of the world seemed to be having
the time of their lives."[15] In *The Sacred Journey*, Buechner writes that
meeting Merrill convinced him that he was not, as he'd suspected,
one of a kind and alone in the universe. After Lawrenceville, Buechner
went to Princeton, the Army, and back to Princeton, while Merrill
also spent time in the Army and attended Amherst.

As recent college graduates, they spent that summer of 1948 on
Georgetown Island, off the coast of Maine, surrounded by other
artists, sharing a typewriter as they worked on their books. Buechner
recalls that the time was filled with "easy, companionable, nurturing,
celibate, insulated days ringing with laughter,"[16] and the books they
produced, Buechner's *A Long Day's Dying* and Merrill's *First Poems*,
launched them both into significant literary careers.

Their personal lives would go in very different directions from
there: "Jimmy gay, a poet, an intellectual, a citizen of the world, and
I straight, a minister (of all things), bookish, and for some forty years
or so a citizen of Rupert, Vermont, whose population hovers around
five hundred."[17] They had discovered each other at the age of fourteen,
when each genuinely needed a friend, but their adult lives diverged.
Following Merrill's death, Buechner was asked to speak about him
at the New York Public Library and felt relief that a prior commitment made it impossible, because "Jimmy and I never knew each
other as the people we grew up to become."[18] Still, there are four
boxes of correspondence between Buechner and Merrill tucked away
in the archives at Wheaton.

Buechner asked Merrill to contribute a sentence to *A Long Day's Dying* for good luck, and he produced a sentence in the same cluttered and tortured style Buechner was employing: "But then as though not sufficiently punished by his slow, melancholy presence for the ugliness of her words, she saw, and managed somehow to recognize, who else was witness to her humiliation, Maroo advancing from the groin of the hall as she had never, for Elizabeth, advanced before."[19] The sentence fits into that book seamlessly. Ultimately, *A Long Day's Dying* is about people not being able to tell each other who they truly are, and as Buechner thinks back to those days with Merrill, he believes he and Merrill were as bad as Buechner's characters at communicating their innermost selves, not because they didn't talk, but because "the selves we were beginning to grow into that summer were still in the shadowy wings awaiting their entrance cues. . . . We still had a long way to go before finding our grown-up selves and true voices."[20]

Merrill's memoir, *A Different Person*, published in 1993, held surprises for Buechner, particularly the revelation of numerous sexual adventures. He never imagined there was so much about Merrill he did not know. Buechner almost entirely avoids mentioning sex in his memoirs and wishes Merrill had done the same. He couldn't understand Merrill's rationale for exposing so much and didn't perceive that airing all of this brought Merrill any peace. "His affairs were legion," Buechner writes,

> But reading the book I had the feeling there had been little love in them, little even of very satisfactory friendship in them, and I ended up believing that, although his experience had been vastly wider and more varied than mine in ways other than just sexually, he nonetheless had missed out on much that it seems to me at its fullest and richest life has to offer.[21]

The literary world is divided on whether or not there is a difference between a memoir and an autobiography (and I am endlessly amused by Charles Barkley's assertion that he was misquoted in his autobiography), but there is a wide gulf between the sort of tell-all book Merrill wrote and Buechner's spiritual memoirs. Buechner focuses on events to get at their meaning, and in the case of *The Eyes of the Heart*, when there are not a lot of events to report, he still finds ample material by exploring his inner world. Merrill told stories that the author of *Telling Secrets* believed were better left untold. Even though this was long before social media oversharing became a facet of modern life, Buechner wishes that his friend had simply logged off.

Merrill, one of America's most celebrated poets and winner of both the Pulitzer Prize and National Book Award, made three phone calls the day before he died. One was to his mother, and a second was to his psychiatrist. The third was to Buechner, who promised to say some powerful prayers on Merrill's behalf. "That is exactly what I want you to do," Merrill said.[22] It was only when Buechner called the next day to check in and was told Merrill had died a few hours earlier that Buechner realized the purpose of the previous call had been to say goodbye. "Each time members of the tribe die," Buechner reflects later in the book, "the self we were with them dies too."[23]

· ✦ ·

As Buechner peruses the Magic Kingdom, his eyes rest on the theological works he has kept. The books of his old professor Paul Tillich are there, along with Tillich's contemporary Karl Barth. Buechner expresses admiration for a recent addition to his library, Marcus Borg's *Meeting Jesus Again for the First Time*. Just when orthodox and evangelical believers draw comfort from Buechner's assertion that he believes "we aren't dead forever because Jesus said so,"[24] Buechner expresses appreciation for Borg, a man considered on the edge or even outside the bounds of orthodox faith by large swaths of Christian believers. Their trouble with Borg was his low Christology and involvement in "The Jesus Seminar," which denied Christ's divinity. Theologian Thomas Long summed up the problem for those who take issue with Borg, writing, "It becomes apparent that he knows the way out (from an intellectually-stifling authoritarian faith) better than he knows the way home."[25]

I can imagine Buechner, who elevated the experience of God's presence over reasoned proof of God's existence, being drawn to Borg's call to move "beyond belief to relationship."[26] In *The Eyes of the Heart*, Buechner expresses admiration for Borg's insistence that the church not forget two of its three macro stories. We tend to dwell in the priestly story of guilt, sacrifice, and forgiveness and overlook the exodus story of bondage and freedom, and the exile story of separation and reunion. Buechner doesn't enter into christological questions here but instead focuses on Borg's insistence that there is more to the Christian story than individual guilt and shame. Yet even though Buechner doesn't address christological questions head on, he steps into them in different ways.

Immediately after mentioning Borg, Buechner talks with Naya about her Unitarian faith. When he asks Naya to tell him about Jesus, she has no answer. She hasn't seen him but is hopeful that she will recognize him if she does. Naya can't speak concretely about Jesus because she doesn't know him. For a writer as calculated and intentional as Buechner, it is hard to imagine the juxtaposition of this exchange with his reference to Marcus Borg as a coincidence.

The next section of the book is also about struggling to see Jesus clearly. By this time in Buechner's career he had not only written about the saints Godric and Brendan, he'd also brought several biblical characters to life in *Peculiar Treasures* and written *The Son of*

Laughter, based on the Jacob stories in Genesis, and *On the Road with the Archangel*, a retelling of the deuterocanonical book of Tobit. It was inevitable, then, that people would ask if he had ever considered writing a novel about Jesus. Buechner wasn't interested—he feared it would come across as wooden and preachy, and he felt he wouldn't be able to capture the time Jesus lived in as much as the way it has been already represented in scores of paintings, movies, and books.

He did try repeatedly to write a novel with Mary Magdalene as the main character, and he reproduces a few pages of it in *The Eyes of the Heart*. He thought using the memories of Mary Magdalene, along with the memories of the beloved disciple John, might be a way to write about Jesus. Buechner started and abandoned the project on multiple occasions, and he finished about one hundred pages before giving it up for good. He sensed he was putting too many restrictions on himself and reducing Jesus in the process. Dancing around all of this—from Borg to Naya to his attempts to write about Mary Magdalene—is a sense that no one has a clear or complete picture of the real Jesus, and once again we venture into "eyes of the heart" territory. Buechner set his incomplete novel in Ephesus, because that's where legend has it that Mary Magdalene and the apostle John lived together in their old age. It was to the church at Ephesus that Paul wrote what he did about praying that the eyes of their hearts would be enlightened, and to see through those eyes is to see far more than what meets the eye. Not all that we see always feels good: as Buechner felt himself into the mind of Mary, her memories of Jesus seemed too painful and precious to fully awaken.

He draws a parallel between the Mary Magdalene story and his loss of memory concerning his father—perhaps the reason so many of those memories are lost is because of their pain. What follows, at the midpoint of *The Eyes of the Heart*, is its emotional core: a series of startling revelations about his father made by Buechner's mother when she was eighty-six years old. "Without warning," he writes, "she launched into an extraordinary aria . . . she told me things she had never told me before and never alluded to again."[27] Later that day, Buechner slipped away and summarized what she said in a journal. Here he reproduces his journal notes, without embellishment or commentary. It is a litany of lost jobs, alcohol abuse, suicidal threats, and painful situations. George Merck, Buechner's future father-in-law, urged Buechner's mother to get Buechner's father to a psychiatrist. His father wound up spending a week institutionalized, and Buechner feels he can almost remember being taken to see him.

Both parents had affairs that they did not hide from each other, and once his father had pushed his mother down in a hallway in front of their domestic help. After the week's institutionalization, Buechner's father had been diagnosed as manic depressive. Buechner's mother couldn't recall what course of treatment had been recommended. She does recall, in great detail, the day of Buechner's father's suicide. Buechner says he listened to all of it without emotion, and she told it without emotion. After winding up, she said that she hoped all this sad talk hadn't ruined his appetite, and they went on— "two old conspirators"[28]—to their lunch.

As he finishes telling this story, Buechner makes no comment. Instead he glances around the Magic Kingdom until his eyes land on a copy of Rembrandt's etching *The Return of the Prodigal Son*, noting that in their embrace it is hard to tell which is the father and which is the son. It hardly matters, though, because it is a homecoming for both. Some readers may wonder, "What's the point?" of another exploration of Buechner's father's suicide. If you have lived with trauma, you know it is never done with you, and you are never done with it. It is precisely because the revelations Buechner's mother makes here were not disclosed for fifty years that the trauma from the suicide kept coming out sideways not only in Buechner's novels but his psyche as well. What might his life and career have been like if she had told him these things before he wrote a version of his father's suicide into *The Return of Ansel Gibbs*? Instead there was silence, and then shaming anger after *Ansel Gibbs*, and Buechner's trauma was buried deeper. Now, over six decades after the suicide, Buechner is still making peace with it and with his father, seeing himself and his father lost in each other's arms in Rembrandt's etching.

·✦·

The other loss that informs *The Eyes of the Heart* is the death of Buechner's brother, Jamie. Thinking of Jamie brings memories of their interrupted childhoods and how their relationship was sealed by their father's suicide and subsequent sojourn to Bermuda. Buechner felt Jamie was never haunted by their father's death the way he was, and one reason may have been because Jamie was more open to his grief as a child: a year or so after the event, Buechner found Jamie alone his bedroom crying about something he said had happened a long time ago. When you are a child, a year is a long time.

Jamie spent his adult life working in public relations for a bank and was a very private person. When Buechner wrote *The Wizard's Tide*, his fictionalized version of their childhoods, out of respect for Jamie's privacy he turned him into a girl named Bean. Later, when he revisited the Schroeder family in a series of poems in *The Longing for Home*, the girl Bean had become a boy named Billy.

As Buechner remembers his brother, Jamie's dark wit comes through. Over the phone, Jamie tells Buechner of his terminal condition on Buechner's seventy-second birthday, and after saying that he expected to die in the next two weeks, he added, "By the way, Happy Birthday."

He then says that he's told his wife "to think of it not as losing a husband but as gaining half a closet."[29] Although never a church attender, Jamie asked his brother if he would write a prayer he could use, and Buechner's prayer was on Jamie's bedside table when he died: "Dear Lord, bring me through darkness into light. Bring me through pain into peace. Bring me through death into life. Be with me wherever I go, and with everyone I love. In Christ's name I ask it. Amen."[30]

· ✦ ·

The losses of Jamie and Jimmy Merrill cast a shadow of sadness, and out of that sadness comes a reflection by Buechner over the arc of his career. This section, which concludes *The Eyes of the Heart*, leads me to wonder if Buechner imagined this was his final book. He expresses regret that he felt freer as a novelist to write about mystical experiences than he did in his nonfiction. He writes that he has "seen with the eyes of my heart the great hope to which he has called us, but out of some shyness or diffidence I rarely speak of it. . . . For fear of overstating, I have tended especially in my nonfiction books to understate," and then he cites four examples from his novels where characters have had mystical experiences—visions of Christ and angels—and says, "They are all of them telling my story."[31] Should this be taken literally? He's fictionalized incidents from his life repeatedly, and he may be telling us that these mystical experiences really happened to him. He has reported less dramatic but still compelling mystical experiences in the memoirs and various essays over the years. Maybe his experiences have been deeper, and, as he says in *The Eyes of the Heart*, he didn't want to "risk being written off as some sort of embarrassment by most of the people I know and like."[32]

For many readers, myself included, what Buechner calls the understatement of his nonfiction is the authenticity and honesty that make his memoirs so appealing. Buechner is an accomplished novelist. He brings a creative, light touch to stuffy theological concepts and moribund biblical characters. He is a highly literate preacher. Yet Buechner's greatest subject is Buechner. He sustains four memoirs (and several other "memoirish" books) by exploring the depths of his life with unusual insight and clarity.

The memoirs also work because they are never just about Buechner. *The Sacred Journey, Now and Then, Telling Secrets,* and *The Eyes of the Heart* all travel deep inside Buechner, but each book points to a reality deeper still. He uses the close of each book to express that. In *The Sacred Journey* he quotes King Rinkitink of Oz saying, "Never question the truth of what you fail to understand, for the world is filled with wonders."[33] With *Now and Then* it's Godric's memorable line that "all the death that ever was, set next to life, would scarcely fill a cup."[34] *Telling Secrets* ends with Buechner saying, "I have bumbled my way into at least the outermost suburbs of the Truth that can never be told but only come upon, that can never be proved but only lived for and loved."[35] He ends *The Eyes of the Heart* in the same way, echoing Revelation 21 with these words about the Magic Kingdom:

> What is magic about the Magic Kingdom is that if you look at it through the right pair of eyes it points to a kingdom more magic still that comes down out of heaven prepared as a bride adorned for her husband. The one who sits upon its throne says, "Behold, I make all things new," and the streets of it are of gold like unto clear glass, and each of its gates is a single pearl.[36]

Although there aren't the life, faith, and career-shaping events in *The Eyes of the Heart* that the first two memoirs contain, nor the emotional force of *Telling Secrets,* this book works its charms in its own ways, and it is the final essential Buechner memoir.

FREDERICK
BUECHNER
AS NOVELIST

WHEN ASKED BY AN INTERVIEWER what he wanted to be remembered for, Frederick Buechner said, "I would choose the fiction."[1] Dale Brown wrote that "Buechner's characteristic themes find their deepest expression in his fiction."[2] Annie Dillard, who has called Buechner her hero and inspiration, writes, "The novels are his masterpieces. We must never get too dumbed down to read literary fiction. Nothing else so inspires."[3]

Yet I cannot number the conversations I've had with people who say, "I love his memoirs and other books, but I don't get the novels." A minister I know, herself an accomplished author, was excited to tell me how reading *The Sacred Journey* changed her life. "I never knew what Christian writing could be until I read that," she said. I asked the follow-up question, "What other Buechner books have you read?" She said, "Because of *Sacred Journey*, I thought I should read *A Long Day's Dying*." As she said that, a look came over her face that was equal parts puzzlement and disappointment. I don't think she's tried more.

I wish she'd keep trying.

One reason Buechner's fiction is especially underappreciated by Christian readers is that Buechner is writing to a different audience in his novels. Maude McDaniel articulated this well in her review of Buechner's final novel, *The Storm*:

> Although his nonfiction has always been more satisfying to me, displaying a depth, feeling, and literary virtuosity I do not always find in his storytelling, his fiction often does a grand job of understanding the very real inability among intellectual moderns (or postmoderns, if we must be reduced to using these virtually indefinable terms) to commit to religious conviction.[4]

The intended audience for the fiction has always been the religiously indifferent reader. This is obviously not the case with books of sermons, popular theology, or even the memoirs. Is it any wonder that the religiously committed gravitate toward the nonfiction? If we liberate the Bebb books, *Godric*, *Brendan*, and the others from the expectation that reading them is some sort of devotional or discipleship exercise and instead simply encounter them as literature, and then judge them on their literary merits, we go a long way toward reading the novels as Buechner intended them to be read.

Buechner could have sustained his career solely as a novelist but elected not to. As a result, we know more about his personal life and religious convictions than the great majority of novelists. There are fifteen or seventeen novels, depending on how you count—*The Book of Bebb* combines the four Bebb books under one cover, and *The Wizard's Tide* was reissued as *The Christmas Tide*.

What do these varied novels have to do with each other? In an essay primarily considering Buechner's fiction, George Garrett concludes,

> One of the things that defines and distinguishes the work of a true artist from that of a skillful practicing craftsperson or a

crafty professional is that all of the created work, no matter how obsessive or various and no matter whether it is heavy with meaning or purely and simply lighthearted, bears the undeniable imprint of that maker. You touch any one thing in any one place and you are in touch with all of it. Another identifying characteristic of an artist's work is that for as long as that artist may live and create, each new work seems to be what all the earlier work was all about. Dark or light, promising or dreaming, the latest work will always be the sum and essence of everything else. Until, of course, it is supplanted and changed forever by the next one. . . . Frederick Buechner is a true artist.[5]

My invitation to those who have come to Buechner through his memoirs and other nonfiction is to read the novels, especially those I've identified as essentials. If you like them, scout out what I say about the other novels in the appendix and choose more to read. You will be rewarded.

ESSENTIAL NOVELS

Godric, 1980

The Son of Laughter, 1993

OTHER NOVELS

A Long Day's Dying, 1950

The Seasons' Difference, 1952

The Return of Ansel Gibbs, 1957

The Final Beast, 1965

The Entrance to Porlock, 1970

Lion Country, 1971

Open Heart, 1972

Love Feast, 1974

Treasure Hunt, 1977
The Book of Bebb, 1979
Brendan, 1987
The Wizard's Tide, 1990
On the Road with the Archangel, 1997
The Storm, 1998
The Christmas Tide, 2005

GODRIC:
A TWELFTH-CENTURY
SINNER-SAINT

S UPPOSE YOU ATTEND AN ADULT EDUCATION CLASS at church
one Sunday morning, and the teacher is extolling the virtues of
a book about a medieval saint named *Godric*. You are told that the
author has used the twelfth-century setting to tell a timeless tale and
has taken the outline of a historical saint's life and invented details
to bring him to life. You pick up the book and are a bit puzzled by
the first line: "Five friends I had, and two of them snakes."[1] Unless
you are a poet or an English professor, you don't notice the line has
an iambic rhythm to it. You just wonder if those snakes are real.

In the next paragraph there are references both to "old one eye"
and "ballocks." If you are someone like me, who grew up in a home
with two older brothers and a father who never had trouble using
colorful language, you know exactly what these terms refer to. If you
didn't grow up in a family like that, you may wonder if those terms
are referring to what you suspect they refer to. You turn the page and
read a description of someone named Roger Mouse, who stood on
the deck of a ship so high "it blew the caps off men who stood astern

when he broke wind."[2] You put the book down and decide you've had enough.

Welcome to the conflicted world of Frederick Buechner, novelist. He gets talked about in Sunday school settings, but his novels aren't typical Sunday school material.

Buechner never thought of himself as a Christian novelist nor wrote his novels primarily for Christian audiences. When his career began, Christian bookstores as we know them today did not exist, nor did Christian fiction exist as the profitable genre it is today. He was a novelist who happened to be a Christian, similar to Madeleine L'Engle, Walker Percy, Marilynne Robinson, and Flannery O'Connor. Unlike any of them, though, Buechner was also an ordained minister, and his ordination created both distance and prejudicial treatment from the literary world. He wrote that book reviewers assumed they knew what any novel a minister had written must be about, and they automatically dismissed the book as propaganda.[3]

Ironically, it was because of the "non-propagandist" nature of his work that Buechner never found an audience in the inspiration aisles of secular bookstores or was placed in Christian bookstores. He was marginalized by the literary world because of his Christian faith and marginalized by the Christian world for a variety of reasons: he wasn't published by a recognized evangelical publisher; novels like the Bebb books and *Godric* contain salty language and subject matter; and his work was filled with searing honesty instead of simple sermonettes.

"Oh wert thou near in truth, or was it only that I wished it so?"[4] Godric asks, and his question is classic Buechner. It's never "Thou wert near" but "Wert thou near?" There is always room for doubt, questions, and a different interpretation. "Without somehow destroying me in the process," Buechner wrote a decade before *Godric*, "how could God reveal himself in a way that would leave no room for doubt? If there were no room for doubt, there would be no room for me."[5]

Although Buechner claimed his novels weren't religious enough for mainstream Christian audiences, I read Buechner and say, "That's how I feel too." As the Episcopal priest Barbara Brown Taylor put it, "Very few people come to see me because they want to discuss something God said to them last night. The large majority come because they cannot get God to say anything at all."[6] Buechner wades into the experience of God's silence and reveals much about the nature of faith. Are his questions too much?

Maybe for some. But I don't buy the popular notion that all Christians are unthinking and closed-minded. I believe the majority of Christians are thoughtful, open, and curious. If you are that kind of Christian, *Godric* is for you.

·✦·

Full disclosure here: I stumbled on my first attempt to read *Godric*. Godric's narrative shuffles between first person and third person. His sense of time is elastic—on the first page he wonders if he's got time straight at all, and as the book concludes, he admits that he has told his story simultaneously from both the beginning and end. The Saxon names such as Aedwen, Ailred, and Aedlward were confusing, and sometimes when fish talked and the dead were alive, I wondered if I was meant to understand these events literally or figuratively. And then there was this: right at the beginning, Godric speaks of his sister Burcwen's heart being his. What was that about? Sounds great if it's about an eventual spouse, but a sister? That's creepy.

Above all, though, the vocabulary was the major challenge. It seemed ancient, but the book had been published in 1980. Today, the unusual but rich use of words is among the things I treasure most about this book. You have to slow down and take a few deep breaths to read *Godric*. The book is not a poem, but it is written in poetic language, and poetry isn't meant to be read in a hurry. This is a challenge in our world of Minute rice and instant messaging.

If you slow down and stay with it, though, *Godric* delivers its rewards. I imagine the lyrical prose as a sort of gate Buechner has put up that keeps the casual reader out. I have heard countless people complain about the language (even the review in *Christian Century* panned *Godric* because of the language).[7] To every complainer I say, "Dare to enter, because there is treasure inside." It only takes two or three chapters to catch on. Just keep reading.

Since the medieval saint Godric was born in 1065, a year before the Norman (French) conquest of England, Buechner avoids any English word with a French/Latin origin and puts only words with Anglo-Saxon roots in Godric's mouth. (Imagine the linguistic dexterity needed to do that!) As mentioned earlier, the book is written in iambic rhythm, giving it a medieval poetic feel. An example of Buechner's care with words and attention to rhythm is found in the correction of an error between the first and subsequent editions of the book. Compare these five words:

First edition: "The rascal Lot had slipped."

Subsequent editions: "The knavish Laban had slid."

This is a reference to Jacob in Genesis 29 being surprised on his wedding night, but Buechner originally got his Genesis characters confused. It was Laban, not Lot, who tricked Jacob. Ordinary writers might correct their mistake by simply substituting Laban for Lot. Not Buechner. Since "Laban" has two syllables as opposed to "Lot's" one, subsequent editions of *Godric* also substitute "slid" for "slipped" so the rhythm works by keeping the syllable count the same. And because of the way the words sound together (assonance), "rascal" becomes "knavish." This is a writer to whom every word (and syllable) truly matters.[8]

·✦·

We'll focus on three questions that open doors into the story. The first is, "Whose account of Godric's life are we supposed to believe: Godric's or the monk Reginald's?" (And, when we ask that question, another question arises: "What exactly is a saint?") The monk Reginald has been sent by Ailred, the abbot of Durham, to write a biography of the holy hermit Godric, who lives nearby. This is fact—Buechner's primary source material was Reginald's 481-page *Libellus de Vita et Miraculis S. Godric* ("The Book of the Life and Miracles of St. Godric"). Godric doesn't feel worthy of such a book and does his best to complicate Reginald's task by telling bawdy tales of peddling and pirating, which Reginald cleans up. Godric uses words like "gadabout," "lecher," "self-seeking," "peacock proud," "hypocrite," "slothful," and "greedy bear" to describe himself. Reginald doesn't tell the story that way, saying that he's left "some small truths out."[9] They disagree about everything, including the meaning of the name "Godric." Reginald begins by saying the name means "God reigns" in Saxon.

> "Fetch me a bowl to puke in," I tell him. He's got him such a honeyed way I'm ever out to sour it.
>
> "Godric will have his little jest," says Reginald.
>
> So then I teach him other ways to read my name. "*God's god* for sure. You hit that square. But *ric* is Erse for *wreck*," I say, not knowing Erse from arse. "God's wreck I be, it means. God's wrecked Godric for his sins. Or Godric's sins have made a wreck of God."[10]

Reginald polishes everything, and there is much back and forth as Godric refutes him. Even as Godric consistently dismisses Reginald, a word must be said on Reginald's behalf. What would we know of Godric, or of the good he did, without Reginald? The truth of Godric's life lies somewhere between Reginald's hagiography and Godric's self-deprecation. As Buechner's book closes, Reginald reads Godric his version of Godric's life. Godric becomes more and more agitated until Reginald refers to him as a saint, and Godric explodes. "Saint" crosses a line and gets us into the theological territory Buechner is most interested in exploring.

If Godric isn't a saint, who is? Godric had visions of Christ, the Virgin Mary, John the Baptist, and Saint Cuthbert. He may have healed a leper. He traveled to Rome and Jerusalem and had a religious experience in the Jordan River. He spent the last sixty years of his life living as a holy hermit focused on prayer and meditation. But "saint" was too much.

The old hermit not only doesn't think of himself as a saint, he seems unable to believe his sins are forgiven. (And he is blind to the concept of self-forgiveness.) In acts of self-flagellation, he wears an iron shirt and wades into the River Wear every day, even in winter. His view of himself is expressed during the time Godric served a mighty lord who had a teenage wife. She points at the floor of the banqueting room and explains that it had been freshly perfumed to make it fit for royal feet. "'What's underneath is turds of dogs and grease and spit and bits of bone,' she said. 'The part you see is fair and fresh. The part you do not see is foul.'"[11] She is saying this to describe her life, but fair above and foul below also describes the way Godric sees himself.

There is something universal in Godric's self-appraisal. Who doesn't struggle with feelings of inadequacy? It's ironic that so many Christians, adherents of a religion built on forgiveness, feel they don't measure up. Not only do we think saints are supposed to be perfect, we think we're supposed to be perfect.

A little exegetical work of those troublesome words of Jesus, "Be ye therefore perfect, even as your Father which is in heaven is perfect" (Mt 5:48 KJV) may help us see where Buechner is heading. The Greek word translated "perfect" here does not carry the English connotation of being flawless or without defect. Eugene Peterson's translation in *The Message* is more accurate: "In a word, what I'm saying is, Grow up. You're kingdom subjects. Now live like it." "Grow up" is very different from "be perfect." If a saint isn't some sort of perfect being but instead someone who grows up into all he or she was created to be, Godric moves very far in that direction during his long life.

In the original edition of *Wishful Thinking*, Buechner wrote this wry definition of "saint": "In his holy flirtation with the world, God occasionally drops a handkerchief. Those handkerchiefs are called saints."[12] When the second edition of *Wishful Thinking* was published, Buechner's "saint" entry had been expanded, going on for three more paragraphs after the line about the handkerchief. In the twenty years between editions, Buechner had settled on saints as his topic, and his thinking had grown. Buechner's later, expanded definition says, "The feet of saints are as much of clay as everybody else's, and their sainthood consists less of what they have done than of what God has for some reason chosen to do through them."[13]

In an essay on faith and fiction included in *The Clown in the Belfry*, Buechner shared some of his thought process:

> Imagine setting out consciously to write a novel about a saint. How could you avoid falling flat on your face? Nothing is harder to make real than holiness. Certainly nothing is harder to make appealing and attractive. The danger, I suppose, is that you start out with the idea that sainthood is something people achieve, that you get to be holy more or less the way you get to be an Eagle Scout.[14]

Buechner realized real saints never described themselves this way and instead identify with Saint Paul's description of himself in 1 Timothy 1:15 as the chief of sinners.

·✦·

A second question that opens a door into the story is, "What sin could one possibly commit that would require sixty years of self-flagellation as penance?" Here's one of several places where Godric catalogs his sins:

> I worked uncleanness with the best of them or worst. I tumbled all the maids would suffer me and some that scratched and tore like weasels in a net. I planted horns on many a goodman's brow and jollied lads with tales about it afterward. I took up peddling as my trade. I cozened and tricked the way a baker yeasts his loaves till they are less of bread than air. I passed off old for new. I let out pence at usury. I swore me false. A flatterer I was. A wanderer. I thieved and pirated. I went to sea. Such things as happened then are better left unsaid.[15]

However, one gets the idea that the sins of his youth aren't what haunt him. On his visit to Jerusalem, Godric goes into the Jordan River and feels the river wash the weight of his sins away: "The Godric that waded out of Jordan soaked and dripping wet that day was not the Godric that went wading in."[16] It is events that happen after his transformation in the Jordan that most trouble him. Instead of having his life divided neatly into pre-conversion sinner and post-conversion saint, Godric's greatest sin comes after he lives as a religious hermit. There is a lot of "when I want to do what is good, evil lies close at hand" (Rom 7:21) in Godric. His primary demons are not found in his many adventurous encounters throughout the twelfth-century world; they are very literally close at hand, at home. As he describes his family, he has a strained relationship with his mostly absent father, a good relationship with his mother, a poor relationship with his ever-babbling brother, and an unusually close relationship with his sister. The relationship with Burcwen, his sister, is where the trouble lies.

The word *incest* creates visceral emotions; we hear the word and shudder. Few can articulate exactly what's wrong with it; we simply know it's wrong. But incest is central to Buechner's version of this saint's life. I've read interviews of Buechner by all sorts of serious, sophisticated questioners including journalists, theologians, pastors, and professors. Not one of them ever asked him why he included incest in Godric's story. Leave it to some college students to do that. In a 1990 interview with students at Seattle Pacific University, the question is put to him. Buechner answers,

> Everything in that book, pretty much, is based on what fact there is about Godric, but that relationship I did invent. I had no reason to think that was true, but it arose so much out of the material that it seemed to be almost an intuitive truth. If I'd stopped to think ahead of time, "What a terrible thing to do to that old man's memory," perhaps I wouldn't have done it. I could easily have made Burcwen a stepsister. But I didn't ever think of it that way.[17]

There are copies of the reviews of *Godric* in the Buechner archives at Wheaton College, and often the reviews have entertaining notes scribbled on them. The notes are occasionally signed "HF," and my belief is they are by Harry Ford, an editor, book designer, and long-time friend of Buechner. Ford reviews the reviews with comments like "Worthy but dull" and "A well-meaning review, but what a state of illiteracy we've arrived at." The *Baltimore Sun* review has this comment typed on it: "Your first and only bad review, the incest has thrown the fellow in a *state*."[18] The reviewer states, "When the author, for reasons of his own, allows the stench of incest into the story, he robs his character of the integrity that is literally his only possession." The review, titled "A Technicolor Saint Gets a Black and White Treatment" goes on to call *Godric* "a still-born child of a book."[19]

This reviewer certainly missed the point of the book. Incest is integral to the book's Christian message. In Godric, this sin pushes readers to confront how much they really believe about God's grace. Is incest too much to imagine God forgiving? Is incest unforgivable? Buechner wants us to confront our visceral reactions, not in defense of the act, but to imagine how far God's grace may reach.

Rather than making a "technicolor saint black and white," Buechner took an unknown saint who, if he existed anywhere, existed only on a few black-and-white lines in some mostly ignored books, and brought him to life in technicolor glory. Nothing about Buechner's treatment of Godric should be labeled "black and white." As Godric himself tells us, "nothing human's not a broth of false and true";[20] we're all fair above and foul below. Godric's treatment of Roger Mouse and Reginald stand as examples. The rogue Mouse is Godric's dearest friend. Mouse cries "*Live! Live!*" and gives Godric "lessons in the art."[21] "Mouse's sin," Godric says, "smacked less of evil than of larkishness the likes of which Our Lord himself could hardly help but wink at when he spied it out in whore and prodigal."[22] There is much more grace for the unrepentant Roger Mouse than for the monk Reginald, Godric's least favorite person. The paradox and ambiguity challenge our tendency to divide the world into binary, black-and-white categories of saint/sinner, good/evil, faith/doubt. Buechner won't let us off that easily. By telling both ends of his story at once, *Godric* illustrates that the pre-conversion Godric is not pure sinner, and the post-conversion Godric is not pure saint. "Nothing human's not a broth of false and true"—and the book's structure demonstrates this truth.

Barely noticed among Reginald's last words that close the book is this line: "There is one of his relics in particular—a rude wooden cross bound with hair which was found around his neck when he died—which is believed to have been most efficacious in the curing of numerous ills."[23] The cross was a gift from Burcwen when Godric left home as a young man. It was made of a couple of pieces of wood and Burcwen's hair. Godric wore the cross throughout his life, wrapping his love of Burcwen around the cross of Jesus Christ.

·✦·

A third question that provides insight into *Godric* is, "What was going on in Buechner's personal life that brought this novel out of him?"

Buechner's memoirs provide answers. In *Telling Secrets*, Buechner says, "Nothing I've ever written came out of a darker time" than *Godric*.[24] As I've mentioned in previous chapters, the immediate problem was that Buechner's daughter, Katherine, had stopped eating. Buechner went into a depression, which he describes as hell— a place of no light, only darkness:

> The psychiatrists we consulted told me I couldn't cure her. The best thing I could do for her was to stop trying to do anything. I think in my heart I knew they were right, but it didn't stop the madness of my desperate meddling, it didn't stop the madness of my trying. Everything I could think to do or say only stiffened her resolve to be free from, among other things, me. Her not eating was a symbolic way of striking out for that freedom. The only way she would ever be well again was if and when she freely chose to be. The best I could do as her father was to stand back and give her that freedom even at the risk of her using it to choose for death instead of life.[25]

It's no coincidence, then, that Burcwen stops eating as we move toward the climax of *Godric*. Brother William describes her: "I fear our sister ails. Some lettuce or a parsnip's all she takes for days on end. Water is her only drink. . . . A radish now and then. She won't have meat or bread. I hear her moaning in the night. I offered her some hare I'd caught. She turned away. She cooks for me but takes none for herself. Her legs and arms become like sticks." When Godric sees her, he says she looked "so lean she could have been a sailor shipwrecked on a raft for weeks."[26]

Godric is also filled with references to the longing for a lost father. When Godric first describes his father, he says, "His face I've long since lost, but his back I can still behold."[27] Godric tells of a recurring dream of his father: "I huddle close to him to turn him by his great cold ears so I can see him plain at last. But Godric's hands close ever shut on empty air, and even in his dreams that face escapes."[28] All of this mirrors what Buechner wrote of his own father: "Within a year of his death I seem to have forgotten what he looked like except for certain photographs of him, to have forgotten what his voice sounded like and what it had been like to be with him."[29]

It was only after *Godric* was completed that Buechner realized how much of his own search for his father had been included in it. He wrote the book's dedication to his father in Latin—*In memoriam patris mei*—thinking it helped with the book's medieval feel. After the book was published, it occurred to Buechner that he used Latin to obscure his father's memory, again in obedience to the unspoken family rule that his father's death was a secret.

·✦·

Although *Godric* contains the reflections of an old man, more doors are opened into it by thinking of it as a book about midlife instead of old age. The book was written when Buechner was in his early fifties, and there is much to suggest he is moving through midlife issues as he writes. Death is a major theme of the book, and while Buechner's daughter's illness and issues around revisiting his father's suicide contribute to this, there is so much about death in *Godric* that one is left to conclude Buechner must be thinking about his own aging and mortality as well. Midlife can be a time when death comes into focus in significant ways, along with regret and disillusionment with one's life to that point.

I'm not qualified to offer psychological opinions about Buechner's level of satisfaction with his life. It is clear that Godric's story is a story of abandoning false selves at midlife: the peddler and pirate becomes a new and different person: "As a man dies many times before he's dead, so does he wend from birth to birth until, by grace, he comes alive at last."[30]

Godric arose out of a crucible of events affecting Buechner at the deepest level: his daughter's anorexia, his search for his lost father, the growing realization of his own mortality at midlife. There are mysteries of God's grace being worked out here, and even the genesis of the book had something mysterious and miraculous to it. Buechner was ready for an idea. (Over the years he had begun and abandoned novels about a fifteenth-century alchemist, a twentieth-century woman novelist, a dishwasher in a New England restaurant, and an old lady in a nursing home.) One day he "picked up a small paperback book of saints and opened it, by accident, to the page that had Godric on it. I had never so much as heard of him before, but as I read about him, I knew he was for me, my saint."[31]

Taken with the idea of writing about Godric, Buechner arranged through interlibrary loan to get a copy of Reginald's biography. Upon receiving it, Buechner saw it had not been translated from its medieval Latin. Buechner's own study of Latin had concluded when he was a student at Lawrenceville almost four decades earlier. Providentially, one of his three daughters brought guests home for the weekend, including the chair of the classics department at her school. "I suppose," Buechner wrote, "he was the only person within a radius of a hundred miles or more who could have done the job, and both evenings he was with us he gave me sight translations of the passages I was after."[32]

The writing of *Godric* came with relative effortlessness then:

> Despite the problem of developing a language that sounded authentic on his lips without becoming impenetrably archaic, and despite the difficulties of trying to recapture a time and place so unlike my own, the book . . . came so quickly and with such comparative ease that there were times when I suspected that maybe the old saint himself was not entirely uninvolved in the process.[33]

The book was runner up for the Pulitzer Prize in 1981, finishing second to John Kennedy Toole's *A Confederacy of Dunces*, an outrageous comic story about a genius/social misfit written in 1963, the publication of which was delayed for decades by the author's suicide. (Once again suicide touches Buechner's story.)

Buechner said, "If I were to be remembered by only one book, this is the one I would choose. In every way it came unbidden, unheralded, as a blessing."[34] Saint Godric blessed Buechner in a dark time. Buechner expanded his definition of "saint" through writing this book and came to see a saint above all as essentially a giver of life. The book continues to give life decades after its publication. Over time, Buechner became more comfortable with the life-giving role he was assuming as well:

> What I am beginning to discover is that . . . in my books, and sometimes even in real life, I have it in me at my best to be a saint to other people, and by saint I mean life-giver, someone who is able to bear to others something of the Holy Spirit,

whom the creeds describe as the Lord and Giver of Life. Sometimes, by the grace of God, I have it in me to be Christ to other
people. And so, of course, have we all—the life-giving, life-
saving, and healing power to be saints, to be Christs, maybe at
rare moments even to ourselves.[35]

In *Godric's* most beautiful and most memorable passage, the old
saint affirms this. At this point, Godric has lost the ability to walk to
the River Wear, so his servant Perkin brings the water to Godric:

> "Praise, praise!" I croak. Praise God for all that's holy, cold, and
> dark. Praise him for all we lose, for all the river of the years
> bears off. Praise him for stillness in the wake of pain. Praise him
> for emptiness. And as you race to spill into the sea, praise him
> yourself, old Wear. Praise him for dying and the peace of death.
>
> In the little church I built of wood for Mary, I hollowed out
> a place for him. Perkin brings him by the pail and pours him
> in. Now that I can hardly walk, I crawl to meet him there. He
> takes me in his chilly lap to wash me of my sins. Or I kneel
> down beside him till within his depths I see a star.
>
> Sometimes this star is still. Sometimes she dances. She is
> Mary's star. Within that little pool of Wear she winks at me. I
> wink at her. The secret that we share I cannot tell in full. But this
> much I will tell. What's lost is nothing to what's found, and all
> the death that ever was, set next to life, would scarcely fill a cup.[36]

Born out of personal pain and suffering, *Godric* stands at the pin-
nacle of Buechner's career. As I have suggested, Buechner is the godfather of the modern spiritual memoir movement as well as a witty
theological writer and effective preacher. On top of these accomplishments, with the publication of *Godric*, Buechner's place as one
of the premier novelists of his generation is secure.

THE SON OF LAUGHTER:
HEELS, LAUGHTER,
AND THE FEAR

T HE GENERATIONAL STORIES OF ABRAHAM, Isaac, Jacob, and
Joseph and their families, which fill most of the book of Genesis,
don't lend themselves to easily digestible moral lessons. Questions
abound: What exactly is the redeeming point of Abraham's near-
sacrifice of Isaac? Or Jacob's theft of Esau's blessing? What is the
object lesson of the midnight swapping of Leah in place of Rachel?
Or Simeon and Levi's murder of the men of Shechem? These stories
have both puzzled and enthralled people for millennia. Some of the
puzzling questions eventually yield to paradox: at least half the time,
God's blessing, promised to Abraham and his descendants, seems
more curse than blessing. Jacob is clearly favored over his older
brother, Esau, upending the rules of primogeniture. Likewise, Rachel
is favored over her older sister, Leah. Blessing and curse. Second son
over first son. Second daughter over first daughter. Genesis is full of
puzzling paradox.

Puzzling paradox, of course, is the field in which Frederick
Buechner was born to work. These are his kind of stories, and Jacob,

part-time swindler and part-time believer, is Buechner's kind of ambiguous character. Jacob was "absolutely made to order," Buechner
told an interviewer, "a natural next step for me. Here was another
wonderful saint. Feet of clay but full of the grace of God. A lifegiver."[1]
Buechner creates a rich interior life for Jacob in *The Son of Laughter*,
similar to what he did with Godric and Brendan. The stakes are
higher here—this is the Bible, after all, and Jacob's life is far more
familiar to readers than either Godric or Brendan.

One reviewer noted the vast potential for misstep in tackling this
material: "It is a bold and politically incorrect endeavor, quite capable of giving offense on the bases of gender, race, ethnicity, ethics,
and religion, severally and all at once."[2] Yet Buechner succeeds. Reviewing *The Son of Laughter*, the writer Annie Dillard said, "Buechner
has taken the grand story of Jacob . . . breathed life into it . . . (with)
writing that sounds as though the writer is holding onto a lightning
bolt."[3] Buechner admires Dillard and highly valued her review.

I might quibble with Dillard's line "breathed life into it." A more
accurate description was given by George Garrett:

> It is by poetry and by spare, precise, evocative details that
> Buechner brings these ancient mythical stories not to life (for
> they have been alive since their first telling) but to newness.
> The spirit of the tales, a network of stories around a great and
> conflicted character, is renewed, pushing the possibilities of
> historical fiction toward something new and wonderful. He
> has summoned up an alien world where we feel at home
> because, in a real sense, it already is part of our memory.[4]

Not only is *The Son of Laughter* a logical next step after *Godric* and
Brendan, it also resembles what Buechner did in *Peculiar Treasures*,
where he takes familiar biblical characters and makes them seem new.
And there is much in the book of Genesis worth exploring and

making new. What sort of pain would live on in someone whose throat had almost been slit by his father on the way to being offered as a burnt sacrifice? What kind of person would your brother have to be to trade his inheritance for a bowl of beans? What sort of person swindles not only his son-in-law but his two daughters on their wedding night? Buechner inhabits the psychological world of Israel's first family with telling results.

· ✦ ·

Buechner had already worked with Jacob's story for years. Jacob was the focus of the first sermon of Buechner's life, preached at Lawrenceville School on May 2, 1954. This came in the period between his conversion and seminary matriculation. Even though it was written before seminary, the sermon is strikingly consistent with the rest of Buechner's career. He tells two stories, the first about the English poet and printmaker William Blake's penchant for visions, particularly Blake's 1793 engraving *I Want, I Want* of a ladder stretching to the moon. (The first edition of *Wishful Thinking* featured Blake's engraving on the cover.) Second is the Genesis story of Jacob's ladder, and Buechner points out that while Blake's ladder was for a man to climb up, Jacob's ladder is one God travels down. He concludes with God's ultimate downward descent in the incarnation of Jesus Christ.[5]

At Union, Buechner had to write the dreaded "Pentateuch Paper" as the climax of James Muilenburg's introductory Old Testament course. The paper was one of Union's rites of passage and had to be substantial both in length and in depth. Although already an accomplished novelist, Buechner hadn't done an academic paper since his graduation from Princeton six years earlier. Buechner focused his paper on Jacob and felt it revolutionized his understanding of the

Bible. For the first time, he saw that the Bible was not the collection of moral lessons taken from the virtues of upstanding characters he'd previously assumed it was. Instead, he realized that holiness can live in people as shifty as Jacob. Muilenburg believed the key to really understanding the Bible was to see it as your own story. Years later, speaking at the time of the publication of *The Son of Laughter*, Buechner revealed how he saw himself in the story:

> Jacob is on the lam . . . (yet) nothing . . . puts us beyond the reach of God's mercy. I think I found that in my own life . . . a lot of things happened to me as a child and as a young man, throughout my life, that might have turned me off to any possibility of being a religious person, and yet somehow or other it did not happen that way. There welled up out of dark moments, confused moments, tragic moments, something holy that drew me to God.[6]

The Magnificent Defeat, the title sermon of Buechner's 1966 volume of Exeter sermons, is also about Jacob. Buechner begins by explaining that Jacob's story is not the sort of edifying story one expects from the Bible. In Jacob's case, honesty is far from the best policy, and there is no sense that Jacob reaps what he sows. He's like the morally vacuous among us who wind up succeeding in life. Except he isn't, because of what happened to him during that long night he spent wrestling with that mysterious stranger on the banks of the Jabbok. "Power, success, happiness, as the world knows them," Buechner told the young men at Exeter, "are his who will fight for them hard enough; but peace, love, joy, are only from God. And God is the enemy whom Jacob fought there by the river, of course, and whom in one way or another we all of us fight—God, the beloved enemy." Broken and battered with his hip out of joint, Jacob limps away, prefiguring Jesus, who also comes "staggering on broken feet out of the tomb toward the Resurrection, bearing on his body the proud insignia of the defeat which is victory, the magnificent defeat of the human soul at the hands of God."[7]

Buechner included Jacob (and Dinah, Esau, Isaac, Rachel, and Rebecca) in the character sketches in *Peculiar Treasures*. Here he returns to the nighttime vision of the ladder and echoes *The Magnificent Defeat*: "The lesson was, needless to say, that even for a dyed-in-the-wool, double-barreled con artist like Jacob there are a few things in this world you can't get but can only be given, and one of these things is love in general, and another is the love of God in particular."[8] When the character sketches of *Peculiar Treasures* were included in *Beyond Words* in 2004, Buechner kept the content of each the same and added another character, Jacob's swindling father-in-law, Laban, to the mix. Laban's addition makes sense—as we'll see, Buechner's portrayal of Laban in *The Son of Laughter* is so comically rich he threatens to run off with the whole book.

·✦·

In 1993, almost forty years after that first sermon about Jacob, Buechner tackled the stories of Jacob as a novel. I find it best to read *The Son of Laughter* with the Bible close at hand. Again and again I'll read something and think, *Buechner must have made this up* only to find it in the Bible. For example, there are the nicknames Buechner uses: Heels, Laughter, and the Fear. The Hebrew name *Ya'aqov* is a variation on the Hebrew word for heel, and in Genesis 25:26 Esau was born first, but Jacob came out immediately afterward, holding his older brother's heel. *Yitshaq* is the Hebrew word for laughter, and laughing is what old Sarah does when she is told she'll become pregnant in her old age. When that promise is kept, the child is named laughter because "God has brought laughter for me; everyone who hears will laugh with me" (Gen 21:6). Ironically, as Buechner tells the story, Isaac is bland and unfunny. The Fear is the name of God, straight from Jacob's lips in Genesis 31:42: "If the God of my father, the God of Abraham and the Fear of Isaac, had not been with me."

Buechner sticks close to the text of Scripture. It's below the surface that he explores layers of doubt and shame, which give complexity to the characters. For example, the near-sacrifice of Isaac is followed quickly by the death of Isaac's mother, Sarah. Buechner adds this musing from Isaac: "When my mother heard what Abraham had nearly done to her son, she was dead within the year. What killed her? You tell me."[9] To the episode of Jacob stealing Esau's blessing from their mostly blind father Isaac, Buechner adds more possibilities than a surface reading of the text gives. Looking back on the incident as an old man, Jacob remembers telling Isaac he was Esau: "I do not know to this day if he believed me. . . . Maybe he knew all along I was Jacob. Maybe though it was Esau he loved, it was Jacob he believed in."[10]

Buechner doesn't invent as much as entice details out of characters and events we already know. How does Sarah look when Abraham is visited and told she'd bear a child? She's described as mostly bald and toothless, with "breasts hung flat as a hound's ears."[11] Since her beauty left her, she doesn't show herself to strangers, explaining why she held back inside their tent when the strangers visited Abraham. Esau, with a name "somewhere between Heehaw and Seesaw," is described in manic-depressive terms: "He was either weeping on your neck or threatening to wring it, either roaring with delight or looking as if he was about to hang himself."[12] Isaac is prone to silence, which his wife, Rebekah, blames on the trauma of Abraham's near sacrifice. Rebekah is a schemer, and she is pulling the strings when Jacob lies his way to the blessing meant for Esau. It's a family trait:

Jacob's trickery comes straight from his mother, but Rebekah's scheming pales when compared to her brother, Laban.

Buechner had a lot of fun writing Laban, who lives by that old saw that you've got to cheat your friends because your enemies will never get that close. "Is Laban a man to cheat his own sister's son?"[13] he asks, and the answer is a resounding yes. On the morning after the night Laban tricked Jacob by substituting Leah for Rachel, Laban says,

> Jacob, I didn't do it. I did it, yes, but I could not help myself. . . .
> Did I say which daughter? I am only asking, Jacob. Did I speak
> the name of the daughter I promised? . . . I mention it only
> because in matters like this the judges of Haran set great store
> by the actual words that were spoken or not spoken. I myself
> set no store by them at all.[14]

He spits out words rapid-fire, full of double-talk and fuss, cheating whoever dares to get close.

The great scenes of Genesis are also Buechner's most memorable scenes. Jacob's dream at Bethel of a stone stairway with angels ascending and descending could be a Buechnerian vision, the sort of peeling back of the layers between heaven and earth that characters in several Buechner novels get glimpses of. Heaven and earth are not on distant planes; they are intertwined and have much to do with each other. For Jacob, the vision comes while he is on the run from Esau, on his way to Laban's. Instead of getting his just deserts for hoodwinking Isaac and cheating Esau, God comes to Jacob with words of blessing and assurance. Everything is ablaze with light—the voice Jacob hears is "Light's voice,"[15] and light even fills his mouth when he tries to speak. God is light, not fear.

A second encounter with God comes twenty years later, after Jacob has become a wealthy man as part of Laban's household. Deathly afraid because he is heading back toward Esau, Jacob has sent his wives and children ahead and spends the night alone by the Jabbok River. He is attacked during the night by an unknown assailant:

> Each time I thought I was lost, I escaped somehow. . . . For hours it went on that way. Our bodies were slippery with mud. We were panting like beasts. We could not see each other. We spoke no words. I did not know why we were fighting. It was like fighting in a dream. . . . It was my life I clung to. My enemy was my life. My life was my enemy.[16]

Jacob gets a glimpse of the stranger's face, and just as at the stone staircase, the face is the face of light. Jacob receives his sacred wound as the stranger crushes Jacob's hip, blesses him, and renames him Israel, because he has wrestled with God and prevailed. Israel is a more dignified named than Heels, but it is a hard-earned name.

At Exeter, Buechner had called this "The Magnificent Defeat"; the respected Old Testament scholar Walter Brueggemann acknowledges Buechner's title as a valid interpretation but also wonders if perhaps "The Crippling Victory" might be more accurate.[17] Brueggemann calls the episode a theology of power in weakness and equates it to the disciples arguing about thrones, only to be answered by Jesus "asking them about cups, baptisms, and crosses."[18]

Broken and blessed, Jacob/Israel limps away to encounter Esau. Twenty years earlier, Jacob had fled home because he knew Esau planned to kill him. How would Esau react now? Buechner names the earlier chapter at the Jabbok "The Face of Light" and follows this now with "The Face of Esau." The reader is to understand that the two meetings are interrelated. Esau greets his brother with the warmth of the prodigal son's father in Luke 15—he runs toward Jacob with outstretched arms. "To see your face is like seeing the face of God,"[19] Jacob says. Indeed, Esau isn't just *like* God, he is behaving as God behaves: Esau has come to his brother in love, not anger. Their encounter is all grace.

As Jacob reflects on the words he said to Esau about his face being like the face of God, he realizes the words have come from his new identity as Israel, not the old Jacob. He is unsure what they mean, emphasizing the paradox and puzzle of these stories. Jacob has died, and Israel lives, yet his new life has come at a cost. He had the power to wrestle with God all night and was seriously wounded in the process. Whether magnificent defeat or crippling victory, Jacob's story raises as many questions as it answers. What sort of grace is this? What kind of blessing? The paradox brings back images of young Buechner's sojourn in Bermuda following his father's suicide— a crippling wound accompanied by blessing.

· ✦ ·

Occasionally, Buechner has clearly added to the biblical story. For example, in Genesis 26 there is a famine, and Isaac is instructed to go to Gerar, in the land of King Abimelech of the Philistines. As Buechner tells it, Isaac has two six-sided stones with signs on them: a white stone for day and a black one for night. The stones had been in the family for generations. Isaac casts the stones to find out why the Fear is angry. (The famine is understood as proof of God's anger.) Jacob is filled with self-doubt and fear as the stones are rolled. He's sure he knows the root of the Fear's anger, because he had recently gotten Esau to trade his birthright for a bowl of mush. The stones reveal the Fear isn't angry and show the name "Abimelech." It's the first of many grace lessons Jacob is to receive. Buechner added the extrabiblical stones to add grace notes to the sojourn to Gerar and to represent the mix of idolatry and super-stition the faith of Israel sprang from. Buechner employs similar de-vices in the novel *Brendan*, illustrating how Christianity grew in Ireland during the fourth century from a similar pagan mix. Of course, because the stones are black and white, they also represent paradox.

Another extrabiblical addition comes as Jacob steals Esau's blessing. In Buechner's version, when Jacob comes to Isaac pretending to be Esau, a white rat sits near Isaac. Jacob receives Isaac's blessing, but "it was not I who ran off with my father's blessing. It was my father's blessing that ran off with me."[20] Unable to look at Isaac, Jacob looks at the rat instead and sees another has joined her. Fantastically, one of the rats winks at Jacob. The meaning is plain enough: the rats recognize one of their own.

A third minor but symbolic detail is added to the story of the rape of Dinah and slaughter of the men of Shechem found in Genesis 34. Jacob is outraged at his sons. As he confronts them, he notices a thread of ants going down into a hole. The image is repeated again later in the book. My interpretation of the ants is that they represent the depths to which Jacob and his descendants are falling and will fall.

· ✦ ·

The rape and slaughter in Genesis 34 is as difficult a series of events to interpret as any in the Bible. Brueggemann writes, "This narrative will surely not be widely used in theological exposition," and says the story "speaks about the convergence of *elemental passion, economic advantage, religious scruple,* and *ecumenical vision.*"[21] Other scholars add strongly that the story is about rape, and the hesitant treatment of it is evidence of the suppression of rape. Buechner explores the passion, excludes the rape, and lightly touches on the questions about economics and how Israel will relate to its neighbors. For Buechner, the main point is that Jacob's sons are not under his control, and the ants plunging into the earth foreshadow not only Joseph being cast into a pit and then sold into slavery in Egypt at the hands of his jealous brothers but also the eventual enslavement of the nation of Israel in Egypt.

Buechner's handling of the events relating to Dinah and Shechem are both moving and disturbing. The Bible is fairly mute about Jacob's reaction to Simeon and Levi's massacre of the people of Shechem, but Buechner has an incensed Jacob tying Simeon and Levi to a tree for three days. When Leah intercedes on her sons' behalf, Jacob weeps for "all the sadness there is between fathers and sons."[22] This is a pain Buechner knew well.

Buechner's disturbing choice is to recast the precipitating event, the rape of Dinah, as something other than rape. Buechner casts doubts on the rape story—he has Jacob imagining the liaison between Shechem (the story is a little confusing because one of the main characters is named Shechem, and the place he lives is also called Shechem) and Dinah as a romantic encounter. However, Dinah's brothers Simeon and Levi are furious, believing that "Shechem had defiled the Fear himself. Our whole people had been raped."[23] What Jacob sees as romance, his sons see as violation. In the biblical text, Jacob is passive about what happened to Dinah. Buechner is offering an explanation for Jacob's passivity.

Shechem and his father, Hamor, come to Jacob to arrange a marriage. Buechner portrays Shechem as a "heartsick boy" instead of sexual predator. The fathers—Jacob and Hamor—are rational and seek to work things out. The sons are passionate: Shechem's passion caused the whole thing, and now, before Jacob can respond to Hamor's request, Simeon usurps his father's authority and leaps to his feet passionately demanding the men of Shechem be circumcised. The men of Shechem agree to this, convinced by Hamor's explanation of circumcision's economic and sexual advantages. While they are recovering from their circumcisions, Simeon and Levi attack them, especially terrorizing Hamor and Shechem as they kill them. The other sons of Jacob follow and plunder the whole city (and rape the women of Shechem). In both the Bible and in Buechner's telling, the men have a lot to say, but Dinah is silent and voiceless. Buechner has her shutting down—she does not speak or eat or sleep and reverts to lying down and sucking her thumb.

While there are few sermons preached on Genesis 34, there are plenty of interpretations. Most commentators acknowledge the rape but then minimize it. For example, one conservative commentary begins its exposition by blaming Dinah, saying her action "loosened a stone that caused a landslide. . . . Dinah's step toward social interaction had serious complications. Avoidance of the Canaanites would have been much safer."[24] On the other end of the spectrum is a plain interpretation that the story is simply about rape, and those who deny it perpetuate a culture that condones rape. Because he offers an alternative explanation, Buechner's interpretation is a "rape-prone" interpretation that travels a different route than the conservative interpretation but arrives at the same minimizing place.[25]

Which is it? Although we tend to imagine ourselves as objective, the reality is that interpreters often get out of a text what they bring into it. Buechner (and the majority of other interpreters) minimize the violation of Dinah in Genesis 34. Buechner had other aims in mind. He uses this story to lead into another challenging story recorded in Genesis 35:22, where Reuben has sex with his father's concubine, Bilhah. (Bilhah was Rachel's maid and the mother of Dan and Naphtali.) All of this is illustration that things are not well with Jacob and sets up the final third of the book, when Jacob's sons rise up against Joseph, Jacob's favorite son.

At least one reviewer mentioned that the novelization of this material was a "politically incorrect endeavor," and Buechner's treatment of the story of Dinah and Shechem reopens the criticism heard when he taught at Harvard, when the texts he assigned were deemed sexist. In addition, Buechner has been criticized for not using women preachers as examples in *Telling the Truth*.[26] He doesn't write from a female perspective; throughout his career, the women in his novels are supporting characters. Novels with main characters as diverse as Mary Magdalene or an old woman in a nursing home were all abandoned.

Similarly, one can ask critical questions about Buechner and his treatment of race. His Bebb novels are marred by the cartoonish characterization of Native Americans, and *Treasure Hunt* features an African American character awash in racist stereotypes. Additionally, Buechner wrote more than a dozen novels in the civil rights era, and none of them deal specifically with race. I cannot help but think of the passages he wrote in *Now and Then* about feeling depressed when he first moved to Vermont and the late-1960s world was exploding around him while he sat on his mountain writing *The Entrance to Porlock*. Did he have a full conception of how privileged he was to sit in comfort while city after city in America exploded in racial violence?

Does Buechner have sexist and racist biases? The answer has to be yes. Buechner admits this in a sermon preached late in his career: "I am as much the product of my own generation with all its prejudices and preconceptions and hang-ups as anybody else."[27]

The record is mixed. On the one hand, *The Son of Laughter* develops the characters of Rebekah, Rachel, and Leah more than the book of Genesis does, and on the issue of women preachers, Buechner has also often said that his daughter Katherine is one of his favorite preachers. As to race, he participated in the historic March on Washington in 1963, and as a student at Union he sought to bridge the racial gaps of his own upbringing by working in Harlem. But the words on the printed page don't lie. One of the games the children in *The Seasons' Difference* play has a name that begins with the N-word.[28] There are the caricatures in the Bebb books. And in *The Son of Laughter* he looks at a biblical story with rape at the center of it and turns it into something else.

Buechner certainly grew in his career—it is a very long distance from the drawing rooms of *A Long Day's Dying* to the seedy Salamander Motel of the Bebb books. As he matured, he was able to write about wider experiences of life. But even when writing about Israel centuries ago, he is who he is. "Write what you know" is the old adage, and what Buechner knew and was able to explore in the Jacob stories was not the horror of rape and voicelessness of Dinah but the devastation of generational family pain.

While looking at hot-button topics like sexism or racism, one also notes Buechner was silent on the Vietnam War, Watergate, and a host of other social issues. He addressed this silence in an interview in 1983, beginning with a story of being at a seminary once on the same day that his old friend William Sloane Coffin Jr. was there. Coffin was deeply involved in Vietnam War protest and the civil rights movement, and at the time he was perhaps America's most famous progressive public theologian. Buechner was asked, "What about you?" and in the moment wasn't sure what to say:

> But afterwards I decided that there are really two frontiers: the outer—concerned with issues such as civil rights, the peace movement and poverty, the frontier where justice does battle with injustice, sanity with madness, and so on—and the inner, where doubt is pitted against faith, hope against despair, grief against joy. It's this inner frontier that I live with and address myself to. And when I feel like justifying myself, I say that ultimately the real battle is going to be won there. So I don't feel

too apologetic about it. The prophets themselves—I'm sounding so defensive!—worried not only about economic exploitation, about the temple being destroyed, but about the human heart. What changed history was not so much what they said about political events as what they said about the suffering servant.[29]

Is the "inner frontier" argument enough? There are times when it comes up short. America erupted in the late 1960s, and Buechner spent his time writing one of his least favorite books: *The Entrance to Porlock*. In the era of the assassinations of King and Kennedy and the horrors of Vietnam, Buechner stayed on his mountain and rewrote *The Wizard of Oz*. It's easy to understand why he felt depressed.

Yet the "inner frontier" is Buechner's subject. He had attended a progressive seminary and taken classes from Reinhold Neibuhr, the foremost American political theologian of the twentieth century. However, politics and social issues never captivated Buechner. His interests were always more psychological and spiritual than political. Although he may have personally held progressive social beliefs, as far as his writing is concerned, he had blind spots on sex and race and admits as much when he calls himself a "product of his generation."

·✦·

The conclusion of *The Son of Laughter*, focusing on Joseph, presents a narrative challenge. How could Buechner keep using Jacob as a first-person narrator when Jacob believed his son, who was experiencing all sorts of adventures in Egypt, was dead? Buechner solves this by presenting the final section as a dream and moves quickly through the material in Genesis 37–50. Joseph's story is even more familiar than Jacob's—it has been the subject of a Broadway musical, TV miniseries, and other popular culture treatments. Again, Buechner stays close to the biblical text. Sold into slavery by his jealous brothers, Joseph rises to great power in Egypt. Eventually his brothers come to Egypt looking for food, and Joseph strings them along for a while before finally revealing himself to them. He is reunited with his brothers, and Jacob is brought to Egypt to live out his days. The nation of Israel is in Egypt, where it will be enslaved, and the exodus that will come is another of the Bible's epic stories, beyond the scope of this tale.

Joseph's rise to power comes because of both his penchant for dreaming and his ability to interpret dreams. He says the dreams choose him, and these words echo the point of the whole cycle of stories. The Fear has chosen his people, beginning with Abraham and then Isaac. Jacob is chosen over Esau for reasons Jacob never clearly understands. Then the story centers on Joseph, victim of his brothers' jealous rage, but what his brothers meant for evil, God used for good. The Fear is working out his purposes and keeping his promises, and those promises are not dependent on the character of the ones to whom the promises are made.

The Fear chose Abraham, and then Isaac, Jacob, and Joseph. The scandal of particularity, the paradox of blessing and curse, the mystery of election, the puzzles of second son and second daughter over first, the earthiness and vulgarity of ancient life, and the shining goodness of grace come through powerfully in *The Son of Laughter*. It is a remarkable achievement.

Part Three

FREDERICK BUECHNER AS POPULAR THEOLOGIAN

T HEOLOGY," FREDERICK BUECHNER writes in *Wishful Thinking*, "is the study of God and his ways. For all we know dung beetles may study us and our ways and call it humanology. If so, we would probably be more touched and amused than irritated. One hopes that God feels likewise."[1]

Buechner is not as dismissive of theology as that quip might suggest. (And actually, the quote *is* good theology—the infinite God is past comprehension by finite humans, and we are well advised to be humble in our theologizing.) I'm using the term *popular theologian* to describe Buechner because he writes accessible theology for a wide, popular (nonacademic) audience. I am classifying six Buechner titles as works of popular theology.

ESSENTIAL POPULAR THEOLOGY

Wishful Thinking: A Theological ABC, 1973; revised and expanded
as *Wishful Thinking: A Seeker's ABC,* 1993

Peculiar Treasures: A Biblical Who's Who, 1979

OTHER POPULAR THEOLOGY

The Faces of Jesus, 1974

Whistling in the Dark: An ABC Theologized, 1988

Speak What We Feel (Not What We Ought to Say), 2001

Beyond Words: Daily Readings in the ABCs of Faith, 2004

WISHFUL THINKING: RENEWING TIRED WORDS

A RETIRED MINISTER MADE ME SMILE once when he told me that a thousand of his sermons were "salt and peppered" by quotes from Frederick Buechner. It is true that Buechner is quoted frequently—Phillip Yancey writes, "I have a hunch, in fact, that Buechner has become the most quoted living writer among Christians of influence."[1] More often than not, the quotes come from one of three "lexical" books: *Wishful Thinking*, *Peculiar Treasures*, or *Whistling in the Dark*.

The books are unlike anything else Buechner published. They are dictionaries of sorts, each with about one hundred entries made up of theological words or biblical characters. The first essay in *Wishful Thinking* is "Agnostic," and the last is "Zaccheus."

The alphabetized order makes finding references simple, and Buechner offers fresh, witty insights on most any topic or biblical character imaginable. Perhaps because he was raised outside the church, or perhaps because of his novelist's imagination, Buechner uses religious language in refreshing ways. "I've never learned to talk about the Christian faith in the accustomed way," Buechner told the *Wittenburg Door*. "I've talked about it in the only way I can."[2]

His years teaching indifferent students convinced Buechner of the need to renew religious language. "There was a time when such words as *faith, sin, redemption,* and *atonement,*" he said in a sermon at Exeter, "had great depth of meaning, great reality; but through centuries of handling and mishandling they have tended to become such empty banalities that just the mention of them is apt to turn people's minds off like a switch."[3] As a teacher and preacher, Buechner felt challenged to revitalize the religious language and concepts his students were numb to. *Wishful Thinking,* published first in 1973, is a concentrated effort at doing that. It is witty and wise, and it alternates between highly quotable one-liners and longer essays. Here are some of the most quoted lines:

- Doubts are the ants in the pants of faith. They keep it awake and moving.

- Envy is the consuming desire to have everybody else as unsuccessful as you are.

- It is as impossible for us to demonstrate the existence of God as it would be for even Sherlock Holmes to demonstrate the existence of Arthur Conan Doyle.

- Lust is the craving for salt of a person who is dying of thirst.

- The place God calls you to is the place where your deep gladness and the world's deep hunger meet.[4]

Originally subtitled *A Theological ABC,* the revised and expanded version published in 1993 carried a new subtitle: *A Seeker's ABC. Seeker* wasn't in the church's vocabulary in 1973, which is unfortunate, because the second subtitle is a more precise representation of the book. Although ripe with theology, *Wishful Thinking* is more an apologia for faith than systematic theological statement. "Faith is different from theology," Buechner said in a speech at Wheaton

College, "because theology is reasoned, systematic, orderly whereas faith is disorderly, intermittent, and full of surprises. . . . Faith is homesickness. Faith is a lump in the throat. Faith is less a position on than a movement toward, less a sure thing than a hunch."[5]

·✦·

There is a twenty-year gap between the first and second editions of *Wishful Thinking*, and the differences between the two editions provide insights into the evolution of Buechner's thinking.

There are surface changes—the language becomes more inclusive as many male pronouns are removed in favor of gender-neutral pronouns. Outdated references to things like train travel are removed, as is the regrettable quip, "Jews are like everybody else only more so."[6] I'm not sure what that is supposed to mean, but Buechner had decided by 1993 that sort of attempt at ethnic humor was inappropriate.

There are also significant additions that parallel other developments. An entry on "Blessing" appears, a direct result of writing *Son of Laughter*. A new entry on "Coincidence" takes up the issue of divine sovereignty and human freedom, and emphasizes again Buechner's belief that life is more than a series of random events. Entries like "Environment" and "Homelessness" mirror emerging cultural issues. The entry on "Saint" is much longer, affected by writing about Leo Bebb and Godric.

Among the two dozen or so new entries is one called "Parents" that Buechner could not have written before writing his memoirs and doing the requisite internal work those memoirs required. What does it mean, he asks, to honor your father and mother when your parents may have hurt as much as helped you? It is a question he has stood on both sides of, as a child and as a parent. His answer comes with the wisdom born from the depths of his experience. He creates empathy for parents, noting that children should seek to see beyond their own pain and understand the pain that formed their parents, "the pain that made them what they were and kept them from being what they otherwise might have become."[7] He ends with a comparison to the priesthood, which remains holy even when the priest is a rat, a comparison that summons up images of Graham Greene's whisky priest, Buechner's literary exemplar for Bebb, Godric, Brendan, and Jacob.

·✦·

The introduction to *Wishful Thinking* acknowledges debts to writers and thinkers as diverse as Blaise Pascal, C. S. Lewis, Agnes Sanford, and Paul Tillich. Tillich's inclusion raises some eyebrows. Tillich had fled Germany during the rise of the Nazis and, through the efforts of Reinhold Niebuhr, had a position on the faculty at Union Theological Seminary when Buechner was a student. In *Now and Then*, Buechner describes Tillich's lectures as "thick with multisyllabic abstractions and philosophical technicalities" and "metaphysical and abstruse."[8] Tillich's dense, highly philosophical abstractions are also easily misunderstood. Sentences like "Thus the question of the existence of God can neither be asked nor answered. . . . It is as atheistic to affirm the existence of God as it is to deny it. God is being-itself, not *a* being"[9] are fodder for those who have labeled Tillich a "Christian atheist." (Google "Paul Tillich atheist" for a sampling.) On top of abstractions like being and non-being, essence and existence, and the anxiety caused by our finite freedom, Tillich's widow published a memoir that exposed him as a sexual adventurer who enjoyed humiliating her. Charles Marsh writes of Tillich, "A half century after his death, it may seem implausible that a philandering miscreant, given to interminable pontifications, with no obvious interest in the

American prospect, had once been the darling of the religious left."[10] Russell Moore simply calls Tillich a "theological supervillain."[11]

So what did Buechner mean when he answered an interviewer's question about theological influences by saying, "I think the one who's influenced me the most perhaps is Tillich"?[12]

Buechner has nothing to say about Tillich's unconventional morality, and one wonders how widely this was known among students. In theological terms, Tillich had drunk deeply from the wells in his native Germany that taught that the historical-critical method had liberated Jesus and Christianity from the naive bondage of biblical literalism, and birthed liberal Christianity as a way to believe in God in a "God is dead" culture. Liberal theology is conflated, at times, with political or social liberalism, but they are not the same thing. Liberal theology grew out of the Enlightenment, removed the miracles from Christianity, and focused on teaching good ideas, social action and responsibility, and hope in human progress.

Buechner, a product of Union Theological Seminary, perhaps America's premier theologically liberal institution in its heyday, is not a classic theological liberal. He believes in too much—he believes in miracles, the resurrection of Jesus, and the ongoing work of the Holy Spirit. In *Telling Secrets* he writes of his great frustration teaching preaching at Harvard to humanistic atheists because preaching, to Buechner, is ultimately about so much more than just proclaiming positive ideas and values. In *Wishful Thinking* he takes on tolerance, sarcastically poking at a college so tolerant it wouldn't let a minister lead an informal discussion on campus. He repeatedly pushes against theological liberalism, but then says Tillich was his greatest theological influence. How do we account for this?

There are several points where their thinking overlaps. When Buechner heard Tillich lecture about the fall of Adam and Eve as estrangement and sin as the willful action of estrangement, it must have resonated deeply. Buechner had already written *A Long Day's Dying*, where none of the characters connect with each other, as a novelized illustration of estrangement. Throughout his career, Buechner returns to the definition of sin presented in *Wishful Thinking*: a centrifugal force that pushes away God, pushes away others, and widens gaps in yourself.[13] *Estrangement* is a good word for Buechner's understanding of sin.

In Buechner's entry on "Religion," he echoes Tillich's controversial statements about God's existence with more clarity than Tillich did. Buechner explains that since God exists outside of time and space, we have no way to conceive of how God exists, because God does not exist as you and I do. Buechner concludes that while saying "God 'does not exist'" may be more accurate, "since it also is bound to be taken literally, it is better not to say it."[14] This paraphrases Tillich, but Tillich didn't have the foresight (or perhaps interest) to anticipate literal readings of his words or to include a disclaimer.

I've heard numerous people say they appreciate Buechner because his writing has given them permission to acknowledge their doubts. Buechner's inclusion of doubt as an integral part of the life of faith comes directly from Tillich, who wrote that "doubt is a necessary element . . . a consequence of the risk of faith."[15] Doubt arises because faith isn't simply agreement to a list of propositions. "Faith," as Buechner writes, "is better understood as a verb than as a noun, as a process than as a possession."[16]

Tillich identifies as a Christian existentialist (with a debt to Søren Kierkegaard, whom we might describe as a theological superhero). Tillich's belief that existence precedes essence is not exactly the same as saying that at its heart all theology is autobiography, but the two ideas are at least first cousins. Buechner first articulated this notion in *The Alphabet of Grace* and repeated it in several ways in *Wishful Thinking*. Salvation, Buechner writes, "is an experience first and a doctrine second."[17] Elsewhere he says, "Mysticism is where religions start. . . . Religions as ethics, institution, dogma, ritual, Scripture, social action, all of this comes later and in the long run maybe counts for less."[18]

Tillich's primary influence on Buechner, however, is at a macro level. It was Tillich who first got Buechner thinking about the importance of reviving religious language. "I am thinking especially," Buechner said, "in terms of his [Tillich's] great gift for translating the ancient religious words into existential issues . . . that's [a] thing I've tried, especially in non-fiction and in a way in fiction, to show that those ancient words—which are dismissed by so many people because they're so bankrupt now and so drained of meaning—to show that they are symbols of a rich and complex human reality."[19]

· ✦ ·

Like Tillich, Buechner's attempt to reinvigorate religious language got him into hot water. In April 1973, concurrent with *Wishful Thinking's* release, *A.D.*, the magazine of the United Presbyterian Church (Buechner's denomination), published excerpts from *Wishful Thinking* entitled the "ABCs of Salvation." A barrage of unappreciative letters to the editor of *A.D.* followed. "Just who, by all that is holy, is this Frederick Buechner?" began one. "If I want to read something witty, I'll peruse Noel Coward or Dorothy Parker."[20] A minister from Akron wrote that the article should have been called "The ABCs of Reprobation."[21] The letters by midsummer came in a volume of six to one against Buechner, whose words were called "blasphemy," "clutter," "quasitheological meanderings," and "tactless."[22] The readers were upset that Buechner said long stretches of the Bible were boring, that he claimed people outside the Christian faith could behave in Christian ways, that he used wit, and, above all, that he wrote in poor taste.

The prevailing wisdom today is that it is Buechner's fiction—especially the Bebb books—that is too wild for conventional Christian readers. But in 1973, at the same time as the Bebb books were being written, his nonfiction was too far out, at least for a Presbyterian audience. The mistake the editors of *A.D.* made was to think Buechner wrote *Wishful Thinking* for Presbyterian ministers in Akron. He was writing for those like the "nego" students from Exeter, Christianity's cultured despisers.

But how then do we explain the ongoing appeal of *Wishful Thinking* (and the other ABC books that followed it) to Christian readers? Consider also the enduring attraction of books like C. S. Lewis's *Mere Christianity* or *The Screwtape Letters.* Apologetic works appeal to Christians. In the midst of a world that is indifferent or even openly hostile to the Christian faith, it can be reassuring to read rational and reasonable statements of the faith. And as in Lewis's books, there are plenty of short apologetic essays in *Wishful Thinking.* But unlike Lewis, Buechner's appeal is primarily to experience instead of reasoned proof. Buechner is, like Tillich, a Christian existentialist. "Almost nothing that makes any real difference," Buechner writes under the heading "Faith," "can be proved. . . . I cannot prove that life is better than death or love better than hate. I cannot prove the greatness of the great or the beauty of the beautiful. . . . Faith can't prove a damned thing. Or a blessed thing either."[23]

Buechner explains the limits of apologetics in *Whistling in the Dark,* his 1988 follow-up to *Wishful Thinking.* He relates a story about C. S. Lewis, who said that no doctrine ever appeared thinner than after he'd spent time defending it. This happens because defense requires reducing faith to a manageable size. "It's easier to hold a fortress against the enemy," Buechner writes, "than to hold a landscape." Along with this, Buechner points out two additional problems. First, "logic and plausibility are not the heart of the matter," and a faith that appears good on paper can struggle to excite in real life. The other trap for the apologist comes from the amount of effort put into the defense of faith. Apologists, Buechner writes, "may end up not so much defending the faith because they believe it is true as believing the faith is true because they have worked so hard and long to defend it."[24]

Buechner also makes compelling arguments, but ultimately his appeal arises from more than just the strength of those arguments. His honesty about the struggles of belief and the imagination he uses expressing it account for much of his appeal. In a rare moment of transparency, Antonio Parr and Leo Bebb talk about belief in *Open Heart*, the second Bebb book:

"Listen," Bebb said. "That's not even half of what I believe."

"What else do you believe?" I said.

"Antonio," Bebb said. "I believe everything."

It was a remark of such classic grandeur that for a few moments I sat there in the twilight silent before the sheer magnitude of it.

"You make it sound almost easy," I said finally.

"Don't kid yourself," Bebb said, turning slowly to where he could look at me. "It's hard as hell."[25]

·✦·

Philip Yancey has pointed to Buechner's appeal:

For him [Buechner], faith was a pilgrimage undertaken voluntarily as an adult, a journey fraught with risk. Buechner's

chronicles of that journey have, almost uniquely among
modern writings, managed to attract readers from two polarized worlds, the Eastern elite and conservative evangelicals. . . .
The fiction speaks to the "cultured despisers" of religion while
his nonfiction, more overt, finds its primary audience among
those already committed to the faith. . . . Frederick Buechner
and evangelicals have gotten much better acquainted in the last
two decades. . . . Appreciation of his craft continues to grow—
who else gets equally laudatory reviews in *Christianity Today*
and the *Christian Century*?[26]

Lauren Winner struck a similar note: "When it comes to nonfiction, evangelicals have adopted Buechner as one of their own,
cramming his volumes onto shelves filled with Dallas Willard and
Eugene Peterson. . . . Buechner, not Billy Graham, is the evangelist
for our time. He doesn't say, 'This is what worked for me—you've
got to do it too.' Instead he says, 'This is what worked for me, do
with it what you will.'"[27]

Yet just as earlier I claimed Buechner is no theological liberal, he
is not a classic evangelical either. There is a humorous moment in
Buechner's *Wittenburg Door* interview when he says he's never heard
of the Four Spiritual Laws. "Bill Bright would not be happy," the
interviewer says. "Who is Bill Bright?" Buechner wonders. The interviewer goes on to describe Bright's efforts to reach the world for
Christ. "He hasn't reached me," Buechner says.[28]

Russell Moore conveys the prevailing theological placement of
Buechner when he calls him "a mainline Protestant from Vermont."[29]
But, as I've already noted, Buechner and the Presbyterians were never
very comfortable with each other. There is, however, one oft-overlooked
and oft-condescended-to expression of the church his theology
mirrors: Pentecostalism. His first great influence in this direction

came from the faith-healer Agnes Sanford, whom he met while at Exeter, and her teaching that Jesus' hands are tied by the weak prayers coming out of most churches fits well with Pentecostalism. Under "Prayer" in *Wishful Thinking*, Buechner writes, "Believe Somebody is listening. Believe in miracles."[30] Prayers that tie Jesus' hands are prayers governed by post-Enlightenment rationality. Pentecostalism embraces more ways of knowing than just rational thought, and opening yourself to a Spirit-filled world opens up other possibilities. Perhaps we're not alone in the universe. In a pithy entry in *Peculiar Treasures*, Buechner writes that while people only see what they expect to see, animals see what is there, and the next time an old horse whinnies at an empty horizon, "we might do well to consider at least the possibility that the horizon may not be quite as empty as we think."[31] Angels fill trees in *Brendan*, and *On the Road with the Archangel* goes into great detail explaining what angels are up to.

Buechner's consistent elevation of experience over reason is also Pentecostal. The assertion that all theology is autobiographical is Pentecostal. "Listen to your life" is what Pentecostals do. Buechner's sense that the Holy Spirit is alive and active is Pentecostal. I am not saying he is a Pentecostal—he isn't—but his openness to miracles and the Spirit shares much with Pentecostal belief. And then, of course, there is Buechner's alter ego Leo Bebb. How do we account theologically for Leo Bebb? What stripe of believer is he? An unspoken determinative factor in church affiliation is often socioeconomic class. Buechner, with his patrician roots and Merck marriage, is a long socioeconomic way from traditional Pentecostalism. Not so Leo Bebb. Although Bebb did not speak in tongues, he has many other marks of Pentecostalism about him. Buechner's own journey with Bebb shares the prejudices many hold toward Pentecostalism. When Buechner created Bebb, he did so thinking of Bebb as a con man and a villain. He wound up falling in love with Bebb and seeing him as a saint because he was so alive and brought life to everyone around him. Indeed, Bebb lights up every one of the 530 pages of the *Book of Bebb* he appears on.

·✦·

Perhaps the safest thing to say is that Buechner is *sui generis*, neither liberal nor conservative, not Pentecostal nor evangelical nor mainline. "Faith is less a position on than a movement toward," Buechner said at Wheaton College, and "movement toward" defies categorization. A concept borrowed from mathematics, the idea of a centered set instead of bounded set, helps. A bounded set has the boundaries of a circle, and a point is either inside or outside the circle. A centered set is focused on its center and doesn't have boundaries. In faith terms, the focus is on belonging more than belief, on direction rather than definition. Some Christians spend enormous energy on the "in and out" delineations a bounded set requires. A centered set places Jesus at the center without boundaries. Another way to illustrate this is the story told about cattle ranchers who realized they could keep their herd together by either putting up a fence or digging a well. Buechner is a "centered set" type of believer. He has no interest in putting up a fence and defining who is in and who is out. He draws meaning and inspiration from a huge variety of religious sources—Agnes Sanford and Paul Tillich are not close to each other on the theological spectrum, but that sort of distance never bothered Buechner.

And in true centered-set fashion, Buechner keeps returning to the center. The Presbyterians may have tripped over *Wishful Thinking* in 1973, but Buechner consistently embraces Protestant orthodoxy. When asked about the Bible in an interview once, he said, "I have always had the feeling that to take things literally may be closer to the truth than some of the more sophisticated ways of looking at the Bible."[32] In another interview, he responded to a question about the Pauline formula of conversion by saying, "As far as justification and sanctification and eternal life, that makes a great deal of sense to me. . . . If justification is the beginning of the whole thing—the moment when suddenly things come right that were not right before—then there is this long gradual up-and-down process of more and more of your life being touched, leading (one hopes) to a kind of marvelous and unimaginable flowering that the phrase 'eternal life' describes."[33] He even defended the notoriously difficult to defend doctrine of the virgin birth in one of his Exeter sermons, saying, "And it will be no ordinary birth, but a virgin birth because the birth of righteousness and love in this stern world is always a virgin birth. It is never men nor nations of men nor all the power and wisdom of men that bring it forth but always God, and that is why the angel says, 'The child to be born will be called the Son of God.'"[34]

Surely another reason for the enduring popularity of *Wishful Thinking* (and Buechner's other works of popular theology) is because although he skates around different edges at times, over and over again he returns to the center, Jesus Christ. "For Christians," he writes in the entry "Hope," "hope is ultimately hope in Christ."[35] Buechner returns to Jesus in several other definitions, among them these:

- To live Eternal Life in the full and final sense is to be with God as Christ is with him, and with each other as Christ is with us.

- Inhabitants of time that we are, we stand on such occasions with one foot in eternity. God, as Isaiah says (57:15), "inhabiteth eternity" but stands with one foot in time. The part of time where he stands most particularly is Christ, and thus in

Christ we catch a glimpse of what eternity is all about, what God is all about, and what we ourselves are all about too.

As far as I know there is only one good reason for believing that he was who he said he was. One of the crooks he was strung up with put it this way: "If you are the Christ, save yourself and us" (Luke 23:39). Save us from whatever we need most to be saved from. Save us from each other. Save us from ourselves. Save us from death both beyond the grave and before.

If he is, he can. If he isn't, he can't. It may be that the only way in the world to find out is to give him the chance, whatever that involves. It may be just as simple and just as complicated as that.[36]

Christ is the center Buechner returns to. He's honest enough to admit the faith he clings to just might be no more than wishful thinking—but he clings nonetheless.

PECULIAR TREASURES: PEOPLE WE THOUGHT WE KNEW

I N HIS FOREWORD TO Jill Peláez Baumgaertner's book *Flannery O'Connor: A Proper Scaring*, Frederick Buechner writes, "Human life is so distorted and distorting that the grace of God is broken to pieces by it like light through a prism and reaches us looking like everything except what it is."[1] This explanation of the way grace moves among O'Connor's grotesque, oddball characters also serves as an introduction to Buechner's take on the men and women who populate the pages of the Bible. There is always more going on than we know. The title *Peculiar Treasures* comes from the King James Version of Exodus 19:5 ("ye shall be a peculiar treasure unto me"), and as Buechner retells the stories of these characters, the emphasis is not only on what treasures they are but on their peculiarity as well. His take fits his own cultural moment.

There was a hunger for new forms of the Bible in the 1960s and 1970s. Stuffy, black-clad, double-columned Bibles were joined by contemporary translations like the Living Bible, Good News for Modern Man, and the New International Version. I remember feeling pretty cool as a junior high kid carrying around my copy of *Reach Out*, the Living Bible version of the New Testament, with its colorful cover and inviting pages.

Peculiar Treasures has that contemporary vibe yet holds up remarkably well forty years after its initial publication. In *Now and Then*, Buechner explained his approach, saying he "tried to scrape off some of the veneer with which centuries of reverence had encrusted"[2] the Bible characters he explores. As with *Wishful Thinking*, Buechner had his former Exeter students in mind while writing. He produced more than one hundred sketches of biblical characters and as in *Wishful Thinking* moves from A to Z, although this time it is Aaron to Zaccheus (the Zaccheus entry here is new, not a repeat of *Wishful Thinking*), hoping to invite religious seekers into the Bible. Again like *Wishful Thinking*, the book speaks to believers at least as much as it does to the uncommitted.

In contrast to *Wishful Thinking*, *Peculiar Treasures* is the first of Buechner's books to be illustrated. It contains a number of pen-and-ink illustrations done by Buechner's daughter Katherine. A few years later, she would also illustrate Buechner's book *Whistling in the Dark*. The art is whimsical at times and complements the text perfectly. I have a clear memory of the first time I read *Peculiar Treasures*. I took the book with me on vacation and stayed up the first night until I'd read it cover to cover. (So much for my week-long reading project!) The language was fresh, and the characterizations were unpredictable. I laughed out loud at some moments and felt a lump in my throat at other moments. I couldn't remember having that much fun with the Bible in a long time.

·✦·

Sadly, the Bible doesn't mix with fun in some minds, and not everyone appreciated Buechner's playful approach. Buechner even expressed some second thoughts about the project, saying,

In that book especially I worry because I sometimes think I went a little bit too far to be antic and interesting. I'm still, insofar as I can imagine the audience, writing to cultured unbelievers who are interested in religion but by no means committed. To catch their attention, sometimes you have to do things that shock the committed ones a little. It is the price you pay.[3]

One review compared Buechner to a "breathless adolescent so enthusiastic about his new and shocking language that he runs the danger of being merely enthusiastic but not true," and even positive reviews can't help but point out that "some of these minibiographies are in poor taste."[4]

The problem for those who worry about good taste and refinement, though, isn't with Buechner but with the Bible. The Bible, in spots, is in poor taste and unrefined. This is especially true in the Old Testament. There aren't many sermons preached about Jael hammering a tent stake through the side of Sisera's head, nor sermons about Onan spilling his semen onto the ground, but Buechner takes these stories on.

My favorite review of *Peculiar Treasures* is tucked away in the archives at Wheaton. Madeleine L'Engle wrote an endorsement letter to the book's publisher, Harper & Row:

> *Peculiar Treasures* is indeed a treasure, and full of treasures. And surely anyone who has thought the Bible full of begats and no jokes will rush to the bookcase after reading Frederick Buechner's book. For those who already know and love The Book, there will be new insights and delights. And above all there is the joy of knowing that God cares about his creation, down to the most foolish and wicked of us. No one can feel unloved after reading *Peculiar Treasures*.[5]

·✦·

It only takes three entries for Buechner to open himself to criticism. He writes about "Abishag," an almost completely forgotten biblical character who appears in the first chapter of 1 Kings. King David, at this point, is so old he is unable to keep himself warm. The king's attendants decide the solution is to put a beautiful young virgin into the old king's bed, and Abishag the Shunammite is chosen for the task. The Bible is quick to point out that they did not have sex. However, this is not noted because of a virtuous commitment to fidelity; it's noted because kings were supposed to be virile. The lack of sexual activity is a failure on David's part and evidence of his decline. Indeed, he will be dead by the end of chapter two, succeeded by Solomon, whose seven hundred wives and three hundred concubines testify to his kingly virility.

Buechner says that Abishag joined David "in the sack" and then says, "By this time, however, the old man was past rising to the occasion. And not long afterwards—perhaps as a result of his unsuccessful attempts to do so—he died." The Bible does not say David was killed attempting to have sex with the young woman, but Buechner suggests the possibility as a comic twist. Maybe Buechner goes too far, but those distracted by his tongue-in-cheek irreverence miss the point that comes in the entry's last line: "This sad story makes it clear that in peace as well as in war there's no tragic folly you can't talk a nation's youth into simply by calling it patriotic duty."[6]

America was still coming to grips with the Vietnam War. *Coming Home* and *The Deer Hunter* were both released about the same time as *Peculiar Treasures*. Buechner was holding up Abishag, who was used and then discarded, in order to talk about what America had just done to millions of its own young people. Perhaps as he wrote this, he was specifically thinking of the young men of Exeter who left his classroom bound for the jungles of Southeast Asia.

Political and social commentary isn't typical of Buechner, so an occasion when he says something with that sort of edge stands out. Yet more than anything, what stands out in *Peculiar Treasures* is not the occasional political foray but Buechner's remarkable wit. When God tells the reluctant prophet Jonah to go to Nineveh, "the expression on Jonah's face was that of a man who has just gotten a whiff of trouble in his septic tank."[7] Writing about the slaughter of Agag, king of the Amalekites, whose story is found in 1 Samuel 15, Buechner notes that "since Agag had hacked quite a few people to pieces himself in his day, he may well have been dismayed by the experience but can hardly have been surprised. What was perhaps new to him was the length to which the friends of God will go to make him enemies."[8]

Sometimes all Buechner needs is one word to display his prodigious wit—for example, when writing the story of Joseph, Buechner refers to Potiphar's "prehensile" wife,[9] and "prehensile" is the *mot juste* to describe that deceitful woman who was rebuffed in her attempts to seduce Joseph and wound up clinging only to his cloak while he escaped.

Buechner's pastoral wisdom and insight are on display as he writes about Barabbas, noting that not only did the citizens of Jerusalem choose to release Barabbas instead of Jesus, but Jesus also would have chosen to release Barabbas: "To understand the reason in each case would be to understand much of what the New Testament means by saying that Jesus is the Savior, and much of what it means too by saying that, by and large, people are in bad need of being saved."[10]

As in the case of Barabbas, frequently the character sketches pivot towards Jesus. When speaking of King David's ill-fated son Absalom, Buechner says, "If he [David] could have given his own life to make the boy alive again, he would have given it. But even a king can't do

things like that. As later history was to prove, it takes a God."[11] In
one way or another, Buechner uses the stories of characters as diverse
as Abraham, Bathsheba, Caesar Augustus, Joshua, and many others
to point to Jesus. Buechner has put cross-references under different
characters to show how they intersect with each other. Most characters don't have a cross-reference; some have two or three. Remarkably, there are more than thirty cross-references under "Jesus."
The formal entry looks at one marathon day in his life, found in
Matthew 8, where Jesus heals various people, including Peter's
mother-in-law, calms a storm, and sends a legion of demons into a
herd of pigs. Buechner is most captivated by the image of Jesus asleep
in a boat while a storm rages. It's the human Jesus Buechner is focusing on, wondering what it might have been like just to be with
him on one of his few days on earth. Buechner knows his portrait is
incomplete—hence all the cross-references, but Buechner understands that more words won't necessarily make the case. I am reminded of how Buechner attempted to write about Jesus through
the point of view of Mary Magdalene. He understands the wisdom
of approaching Jesus indirectly. For example, there are four stirring
portraits of Jesus in *Peculiar Treasures* under the headings of
"Matthew," "Mark," "Luke," and "John the Evangelist." Because
"none of the things people have found to call him has ever managed
to say it quite right,"[12] Buechner's writing about Jesus is strongest
when he approaches from an angle.

·✦·

For me, the two most moving entries in *Peculiar Treasures* are "Job"
and "Judas." "Job" gets at theodicy—the question of why evil exists
if God is good. Buechner has been haunted by this question since
that fateful day in 1936 when his father ended his own life. Theodicy

is also behind the speculations I've addressed in previous chapters about the relationship between divine sovereignty and human freedom. It is the question animating Buechner's essay "Adolescence and the Stewardship of Pain" (an essay that helped me make sense of life following my fiancée's stroke). It is a fundamental question for Buechner, one he returns to over and over.

One simple way to answer the question is to deny the existence of God, which many have done in the face of human suffering. Others stake out ground in the middle, asserting that God's power must be limited in some way because the God of love couldn't be associated in any way with horrible events. The most difficult position to hold is the orthodox position that God is all powerful and all good, yet terrible things still happen.

The book of Job is as ancient as any part of Scripture, which means the Hebrew people wrestled with this problem for hundreds and hundreds of years (and didn't need either the Greek philosophers or the Enlightenment to shed light on this logical challenge to their faith). Buechner's fascination with Job is evidenced by this entry being the longest in *Peculiar Treasures*. He sticks closely to the text, relating the suffering of Job and the bad advice from Job's friends. Along the way he asks the theodicy question: Why had God let this happen? God's ultimate answer to Job is not an explanation at all but a visitation—there is a theophany, and God shows up. He asks Job a number of questions designed to put Job into his place. Where were you, God asks, when I laid out the universe? The questions are effective because a chastened Job then repents. Buechner summarizes Job's concluding thoughts and feelings:

> As for the children he had lost when the house blew down, not
> to mention all his employees, he never got an explanation
> about them because he never asked for one, and the reason he

never asked for one was that he knew that even if God gave him one that made splendid sense out of all the pain and suffering that had ever been since the world began, it was no longer splendid sense that he needed because with his own eyes he had beheld, and not as a stranger, the one who in the end clothed all things, no matter how small or confused or in pain, with his own splendor.

And that was more than sufficient.[13]

In the end, no answer will ever satisfy. Because no answer will suffice, what we need is what Job got: God's presence.

This is the realm not of reason but of paradox and mystery. It's similar to the affirmation Buechner made when writing about his sense of mortality and death for the *Christian Century*:

> We find by losing. We hold fast by letting go. We become something new by ceasing to be something old. This seems to be close to the heart of that mystery. I know no more now than I ever did about the far side of death as the last letting-go of all, but I begin to know that I do not need to know and that I do not need to be afraid of not knowing. God knows. That is all that matters.[14]

·✦·

Buechner's take on Judas surprises by being sympathetic. He humanizes Judas. One way to understand this is to remember Buechner's admiration for Anthony Trollope and the passage in *The Eyes of the Heart*, where Buechner notes that Trollope understood people too well to create one-dimensional villains. If Buechner's novels share anything with those of his literary hero Trollope, it is this: like Trollope's, none of Buechner's novels have real villains in them. Both

Buechner and Trollope want us to remember that every one of their characters is a human being.

Who remembers Judas as human? Judas is the New Testament's villain who betrays Jesus under the cover of darkness with a kiss. But Buechner speculates about a few possible reasons why Judas would have betrayed Jesus. Then he wonders about the reasons for the suicide. Citing an obscure early church tradition, Buechner suggests that Judas committed suicide out of hope instead of despair. Knowing he was damned, perhaps Judas counted on God's mercy after death; perhaps "Hell might be the last chance he'd have of making it to heaven." Could that be possible? Who are we to pronounce the limits of God's grace? Imagining Jesus descending to hell and meeting Judas, Buechner writes, "It's a scene to conjure with. Once again they met in the shadows, the two old friends, both of them a little worse for wear after all that had happened, only this time it was Jesus who was the one to give the kiss, and this time it wasn't the kiss of death that was given."[15]

There's no way to know, but I wonder if Buechner would see Judas with that much compassion if his world had not come apart with his father's suicide. And putting Buechner's speculations about Judas alongside the story of Job, there is a thread that connects both. In both cases it's God's presence that matters. And it's God's presence that ultimately matters for us as well.

.✦.

The last words of the Zaccheus entry capture the spirit of *Peculiar Treasures:*

> Like Zaccheus, they're all of them peculiar as Hell, to put it quite literally, and yet you can't help feeling that, like Zaccheus, they're all of them somehow treasured too. Why are they

treasured? Who knows? But maybe you can say at least this about it—that they're treasured less for who they are and for what the world has made them than for what they have it in them at their best to be because ultimately, of course, it's not the world that made them at all. "All the earth is mine!" says Yahweh, "and all that dwell therein," adds the Twenty-fourth Psalm, and in the long run, presumably, that goes for you and me too.[16]

It's Yahweh that made all of us, and "Yahweh" is the penultimate entry in *Peculiar Treasures*. Buechner lists some of the odd ducks of the Bible like the Queen of Sheba, Jael, and Herod, along with figures as disparate as Groucho Marx, Genghis Khan, and Warren Gamliel Harding, and notes that God not only created them but pursues them as well. He adds that there is a lot of work to be done, but that "for reasons best known to himself Yahweh apparently treasures the whole three-ring circus, and every time we say 'Thy kingdom come,' it's home we're talking about, our best, last stop."[17]

Buechner learned from Muilenburg that the Bible is most real when we see ourselves in it. You and I are part of the "three-ring circus" as well, both created and pursued by a loving God. In the beginning of *Peculiar Treasures*, Buechner explains he started this book with the same spirit he wrote *Wishful Thinking*, aiming to shake the dust off "a lot of the moth-eaten old saints, prophets, potentates and assorted sinners who roam through the pages of the Bible, but what I got for my presumption was exactly the reverse. Who did I think was moth-eaten? They were the ones who shook the dust off me."[18] In the midst of that dust-shaking, Buechner's loving treatment of these characters makes *Peculiar Treasures* an essential.

Part Four

FREDERICK BUECHNER AS PREACHER

For the pulpit is ever this earth's foremost part; all the rest comes in its rear; the pulpit leads the world. From thence it is the storm of God's quick wrath is first descried, and the bow must bear the earliest brunt. From thence it is the God of breezes fair or foul is first invoked for favorable winds. Yes, the world's a ship on its passage out, and not a voyage complete; and the pulpit is its prow.

—HERMAN MELVILLE

MELVILLE GOT IT RIGHT. The faith of the church is that the gospel of Jesus Christ proclaimed in local congregations is the hope of the world, and preaching is the foremost activity of the church. The world's a ship on its passage out, and the pulpit is its foremost part.

Frederick Buechner is a remarkable preacher. He's published several of his sermons and an important book on preaching. What we miss, though, in reading about Buechner the preacher is *hearing* Buechner the preacher. Preaching is an oral art, and Buechner's delivery, with his mannered eastern tone and flawless diction, is special. Fortunately, many of Buechner's messages are easily accessible online. There is a rich treasury of Buechner messages at frederickbuechner .com as well as other sites on the internet.

ESSENTIAL SERMONS

Telling the Truth: The Gospel as Tragedy, Comedy, and Fairy Tale, 1977

Secrets in the Dark: A Life in Sermons, 2006

OTHER COLLECTIONS OF (MOSTLY) SERMONS

The Magnificent Defeat, 1966

The Hungering Dark, 1969

A Room Called Remember: Uncollected Pieces, 1984

The Clown in the Belfry: Writings on Faith and Fiction, 1992

TELLING THE TRUTH: TEARS WITH GREAT LAUGHTER

T HERE IS A MAN AT MY CHURCH who has disabilities from the Vietnam War. He sits in the front row and sometimes has trouble standing or sitting at the appropriate moment. One Sunday morning something amused him during the passing of the peace. As the congregation took their seats, he started to laugh, and his laughter filled the sanctuary. The pastor came down from the chancel to gently help him sit down. She smiled broadly when she was told what he was laughing about, and there was a moment when it looked like she might start laughing uncontrollably too. The congregation seemed more bemused than irritated, and there was another moment when it seemed possible the whole place might erupt in laughter. The moment passed—the man sat down, the minister went back to her pulpit, and the service went on.

But there was that moment, a moment when we almost burst into laughter. I think of that moment in relation to Buechner's book about preaching, *Telling the Truth: The Gospel as Tragedy, Comedy, and Fairy Tale*. Originally delivered as the Beecher lectures at Yale,

Telling the Truth contemplates both the content of the gospel and the preacher's formidable task in communicating it.

It's tempting to call that moment in my own church "the gospel as comedy." Actually, it's probably closer to what Buechner means by the gospel as fairy tale, which I consider the most inspired section of an inspired book. That moment in church was a glimpse of the deep-down goodness and joy that lies beneath all things.

Telling the Truth is the book that launched my journey with Frederick Buechner. I was taken off-guard immediately as Buechner jumps in with a description of Henry Ward Beecher, awash in scandal, cutting himself shaving and writing the text of the inaugural Beecher lecture in blood. Then I was absolutely hooked by Buechner's account of Pontius Pilate resolving to quit smoking the morning of that memorable day he met Jesus. Buechner inserts several anachronisms in Pilate's story: although Pilate is a three-pack-a-day man, he has read the surgeon general's warning and taken it to heart; he is driven to his office in a limousine; he talks to his wife (who is subject to troubling dreams) on the phone . . . and then in the middle of Pilate's ordinary day, an upcountry messiah is brought in for questioning. Before he can stop himself, Pilate has lit a cigarette, and when this man with the split lip and swollen eye tells Pilate, "I've come to bear witness to the truth," Pilate "takes such a deep drag on his filter tip that his head swims and for a moment he's afraid he may faint."[1]

Rather than ask us to imagine the togas and laurel wreaths of Pilate's day, Buechner brings Pilate into our day and makes him seem like someone we know. Pilate is our stand-in as he asks the question we all ask: "What is truth?" In response, the man with the split lip and swollen eye "doesn't say a blessed thing. Or else his not saying anything, that is the blessed thing."[2]

Barbara Brown Taylor was in the crowd in the Marquand Chapel at Yale Divinity School when Buechner delivered his four Beecher lectures that became *Telling the Truth.* Reminiscing about that first exposure to Buechner in remarks made at Washington's National Cathedral in 2006, Taylor said, "Dear Mr. Buechner, you rearranged the air."[3] Taylor is not alone. The slim volume (fewer than one hundred pages) of Buechner's Beecher lectures has had profound effects. For example, Leonard Allen, reviewing in *The Christian Century*, recounts being unable to restrain himself from following his wife "around the house, book in hand, subjecting her to a barrage of sustained eloquence."[4] Herman Ridder encouraged laypeople to read the book, writing, "Were you to assume that this is a book for preachers only, you might miss the most joy-filled, hilarious sermonizing of your whole Christian life."[5] Ridder's point is significant. Even though the book has been a standard text in preaching classes for years, it is not just a book for preachers. It's a book for anyone interested in the gospel.

The subtitle, *Tragedy, Comedy, and Fairy Tale,* leads us to believe that Buechner has divided proclamation of the gospel into three categories. But he gave four lectures at Yale, and there are four sections to this book. A more accurate division is "silence, tragedy, comedy, fairy tale." Each section is important.

SILENCE

Jesus answered Pilate with silence. In the same way, when we come to church asking about the truth, "the preacher would do well to answer us also with silence . . . not an ordinary silence, silence as nothing to hear, but silence that makes itself heard."[6]

Buechner weaves in *King Lear* and uses the closing lines, "The weight of this sad time we must obey / Speak what we feel, not what we ought to say," as a guide for preachers. Preachers must eventually break the silence, and when they do, their task is simple: say what they feel, not what they think they ought to say. In other words, tell the truth. Preachers who tell the truth about their experience of life in all its complexity let the congregation know they are alive and know what it means to love, suffer, wonder, and be delighted. Buechner paints a picture of an average congregation: old ladies with their hearing aids, a young mother giving her child a Lifesaver and magic marker, a college student there against his will, a banker contemplating suicide, a gay high school math teacher who keeps his sexuality a secret . . . and then throws Pontius Pilate, Henry Ward Beecher, and King Lear into the congregation for good measure. They sit in silence, waiting.

> The preacher pulls the little cord that turns on the lectern light and deals out his notecards like a riverboat gambler. The stakes have never been higher. Two minutes from now he may have lost his listeners completely to their own thoughts, but at this minute he has them in the palm of his hand. The silence in the shabby church is deafening because everybody is listening to it. Everybody is listening including even himself. Everybody knows the kind of things he has told them before and not told them, but who knows what this time, out of the silence, he will tell them?
>
> Let him tell them the truth. Before the Gospel is a word, it is silence. It is the silence of their own lives and of his life.[7]

Silence was the theme that initially "rearranged the air" for Barbara Brown Taylor when Buechner gave these lectures. Is it any wonder, then, that when she delivered the Beecher lectures twenty years after Buechner, her messages were titled, "Famine in the Land: Homiletical Restraint and the Absence of God," later published as *When God Is Silent*?

TRAGEDY

The painful reality of sin, of living in a fallen world, means that before the gospel is good news, it is bad news. Buechner makes this point by going to *King Lear* again, reproducing a scene he wrote in *Open Heart* where *Lear* comes alive in the classroom of Antonio Parr (the narrator of the Bebb books), and a humdrum day is transformed as his all-too-average students come face to face with the realization that *they* are the poor, naked wretches Lear speaks of.[8]

Buechner's model for preaching is exactly the sort of exchange that happened in Antonio Parr's classroom, where "the pelting of the pitiless storm" is given its full due, because the news is "bad before it is good . . . tragedy before it is comedy because it strips us bare in order ultimately to clothe us."[9]

Buechner gives several biblical examples. The first comes with Jesus' familiar words, "Come unto me, all ye who labor and are heavy laden" (Mt 11:28 KJV). Buechner instructs the preacher to stop there, before "and I will give you rest." Stop and let the tragic word linger— we are all poor, naked wretches who labor and are heavy laden. The pressure on the preacher is to speak words of comfort, to say, "I will give you rest" without telling the truth about the tragedy of life. But the congregant contemplating suicide, the congregant wracked with guilt about his sexuality, the congregant who masks her fear of life behind a fear of death—all these people need a preacher honest enough to acknowledge and recognize their pain. Yes, joy is the last word, but the first word—the tragic word—needs to be spoken before that.

The second biblical example is Jesus weeping at the tomb of his friend Lazarus. This scene is often sentimentalized when we focus solely on the emotion of it and ignore its harsh reality. Why didn't Jesus go to Lazarus when he learned Lazarus was sick? When the crowd whispered, "Could not he who opened the eyes of the blind man have kept this man from dying?" (John 11:37), they were perhaps vocalizing a thought Jesus had already had. When both Martha and Mary successively said, "Lord, if you had been here, my brother would not have died," the reality is either Jesus could not have saved Lazarus or, Buechner writes, "if *could not* is not a verb that you can make God the subject of, then *would not* or at least *did not.*"[10] That's the reality, the hard truth, of the story. A lot will happen eventually, but the first reality is that when Lazarus needed him, Jesus wasn't there. Jesus' friend died as a result, and Jesus wept.

The tragedy of life the preacher must tell the truth about, then, is not just that bad things happen, but that when the bad things happen, God appears to be absent or at least silent. Jesus experienced this on the cross. "*Eli, Eli, lema sabachthani,*" Jesus cries—among the few words of Jesus remembered in the original language he spoke because, Buechner says, "having once heard them, they could never forget them no matter how hard they tried, and probably they tried hard and often."[11]

The preacher unwilling to acknowledge the congregation's experience of tragedy and emptiness and the absence of God "becomes like the captain of a ship who is the only one aboard who . . . does not know that the waves are twenty feet high and the decks awash . . . so that anything else he tries to say by way of hope and comfort and empowering becomes suspect."[12]

As Buechner explores this, he mentions again pieces of literature he holds particularly high in his canon, starting with *King Lear.* Here he refers to *Lear* as a homily on 1 Corinthians 1:27–28: "God chose what is foolish in the world to shame the wise; God chose what is weak in the world to shame the strong; God chose what is low and despised in the world, things that are not, to reduce to nothing things that are." Those verses are ripe with Buechnerian paradox. Following hard on the heels of *Lear* are other Buechner standards: *The Brothers Karamazov*, *Moby Dick*, and *The Wreck of the Deutschland*, by Gerard Manley Hopkins. Light is coming; indeed, the light shines in the darkness, and the darkness does not put it out. But the preacher who avoids the darkness does not tell the truth.

COMEDY

Describing his conversion in an interview, Buechner said,

> That phrase "great laughter" was my Damascus road for reasons I to this day can't altogether understand. I think part of the laughter is the laughter of incredulity. Can it be true? Can it be true? Can it be true what they say? That there really is a God and that he was in Jesus and he loves us and forgives us and will make all things right again? That he really made the world, he loves the world, he will save the world in the long run? Can that be true? I can only laugh.[13]

Is it true? The question is Karl Barth's, from *The Word of God and the Word of Man*. Buechner initially recognized it as *the* question of the "negos" at Exeter, and it is the question that has guided his approach to preaching throughout his career. Woe to the preacher who doesn't recognize that this question is always in the forefront of the mind of the congregation. And if it is true—if the impossible and implausible gospel actually is true—then the gospel, though it begins in silence and speaks a word of tragedy, ultimately is comedy.

Buechner begins this section with Sarah laughing outside her tent at the suggestion that she is going to have a baby in her old age. Buechner contemporizes Sarah and Abraham similarly to how he treated Pontius Pilate, putting them in a nice suburban home with all the comforts and an empty room equipped with a crib and bassinet for the children that never come. As in the case of Pilate, instead of asking us to imagine life thousands of years ago, Buechner brings Abraham and Sarah into our day, and we feel the pain and emptiness of their infertility. Long after the dream of children had died, ninety-year-old Sarah and one-hundred-year-old Abraham are promised a child. The promise is so ridiculous, so preposterous, that there is nothing to do but laugh. As Buechner put it in *Wishful Thinking*, "They laughed because they knew only a fool would believe that a woman with one foot in the grave was soon going to have her other foot in the maternity ward."[14] They laughed so hard they fell on their faces, and God was in on the joke, instructing the old couple to name their son "Laughter."

Comedy is all about surprise, Buechner says, and our laughter comes from a place as deep as the place our tears come from, "except that it comes not as an ally of darkness but as its adversary, not as a symptom of darkness but as its antidote."[15] The Bible is filled with unforeseeable stories: among them freewheeling Jacob being chosen over predictable Esau, the murderer Moses saving his people, drunken Noah saving creation, and "David the king stripping himself down to his fig leaf . . . dancing like a mad man."[16]

These are all stories of grace, and grace is comedy because it is undeserved, unearned and unearnable, and unforeseeable. Paul called it "foolishness" (1 Cor 1:23), and when Jesus finishes "Come to me" in Matthew 11:28 with "and I will give you rest," it is high comedy. Jesus' whole life can be read in comic terms. He was constantly misunderstood by Peter and the others closest to him, and he was ultimately crucified for all the wrong reasons; crucified as a nationalist revolutionary "when the only revolution he is after," Buechner says, "is a revolution of the human heart."[17] Even the resurrection has comic moments when the ones who should have believed initially dismiss the reports of the empty tomb as an "idle tale," and Mary Magdalene thinks Jesus is the gardener.

And then there are the parables, which are also jokes of a sort. Like jokes, they really don't work if you have to explain them. These are not, Buechner says, the sort of jokes preachers tell to warm the crowd up on a Sunday morning. Parables are different kinds of jokes: "The kind of joke Jesus told when he said it is . . . harder for a rich person to enter Paradise than for Nelson Rockefeller to get through the night deposit slot of the First National City Bank."[18]

Jesus spoke in unexpected ways, never laying out doctrine or the plan of salvation but using metaphor and imagery to speak of the kingdom of God. We dress God up, but Jesus said he's like a man already in bed for the night who tells his neighbor ringing his doorbell to get lost and then "finally staggers downstairs with his hair in his eyes and his bathrobe on inside out and gives him what he wants just to be shot of him."[19]

Buechner not only tells preachers what to do, he demonstrates how to do it. There is a contagious vitality in the way he writes biblical characters and scenes. He speaks of how Jesus used metaphor and imagery and then fills these pages with metaphor and imagery. For example, the lazy servant in the parable of the talents in Matthew 25 sat on his one talent "like an old grad on a hot water bottle at the fifty-yard line on a chilly October Saturday."[20] Buechner never actually says "up your game" or "use words better," but he is doing just that throughout the Beecher lectures. The book version is even printed without the type justified on the right side, evoking the look of poetry on the page, sending a subconscious message about the importance of word choice and creative language for the preacher. On every page he models what it means to use our imaginations.

FAIRY TALE

In a book full of surprises, Buechner's treatment of fairy tale is the
biggest. There is plenty of tragedy in the world, and since in classical
dramatic terms the flip side of tragedy is comedy, that idea is
somewhat predictable. But fairy tale?

Buechner begins this section with the words "Once upon a time"
but quickly says that those words are just another way of saying
"beyond time," a theme he will pick up in *The Sacred Journey.* "Beyond
time" is a different sort of time, the kind timepieces don't keep track
of. He draws on an essay by J. R. R. Tolkien called "On Fairy Stories,"
particularly Tolkien's line that fairy tales provide "a fleeting sense of
Joy, Joy beyond the walls of the world, poignant as grief."[21]

The world of fairy tales is usually not hard to reach—all it takes is
staring into a looking glass or hiding in a wardrobe during a game
of hide and seek. "You enter the extraordinary by way of the ordinary," Buechner says, and once there, "it is a world full of darkness
and danger and ambiguity"[22] where nothing is apt to be what it
seems. The regal woman on the sleigh offering Turkish Delight is the
White Witch who holds Narnia in her grasp; the nice woman in the
gingerbread cottage in the forest is a witch who eats children for
supper. The hero is on a quest, and the story's ending includes both
transformation and revelation: the ugly duckling becomes a swan,
the fierce beast a handsome prince, and the beautiful queen a terrible
witch. There is a battle raging, full of shocks and surprises, but ultimately the battle will be won by good. Joy happens, but here
Buechner digs deeper into Tolkien by tempering the joy: there is
nuance to the victory, it is "poignant as grief," and while we glimpse
joy, the world often remains dark.

Buechner then turns from the make-believe world of the fairy tale
to our world:

You wake up on a winter morning and pull up the shade, and what lay there the evening before is no longer there—the sodden gray yard, the dog droppings, the tire tracks in the frozen mud, the broken lawn chair you forgot to take in last fall. All this has disappeared overnight, and what you look out on is not the snow of Narnia but the snow of home, which is no less shimmering and white as it falls. The earth is covered with it, and it is falling still in silence so deep that you can hear its silence. . . . Unless the child in you is entirely dead, it is snow, too, that can make the heart beat faster when it catches you by surprise that way, before your defenses are up. It is snow that can awaken memories of things more wonderful than anything you ever knew or dreamed.

If you still have something more than just eyes to see with, the world can give you these glimpses as well as fairy tales can.[23]

Here and there we get glimpses, Buechner says repeatedly, echoing Paul Tillich's "here and there in the world and now and then in ourselves there is a new creation," which will inspire much of Buechner's memoir, *Now and Then*.

Like the fairy tale world, the world of the gospel also is a world in which a battle between good and evil rages. Like the fairy tale world, good will ultimately triumph. There is one major difference between the fairy tale world and the world of the gospel, though: the gospel's claim is that it is true, "that it not only happened once upon a time," Buechner says, "but has kept on happening ever since and is happening still. . . . Once upon a time is this time, now, and here."[24]

The job of the preacher, then, is to "tell the truth of the Gospel in its highest and wildest and holiest sense."[25] This seems like the logical place to stop. Buechner has made his point about how glimpses of grace break into our world. "That is the gospel," he says, "this meeting of darkness and light and the final victory of light."[26] However, Buechner has one more trick up his sleeve.

He goes back to *the* fairy tale of his youth, *The Wizard of Oz.* Knowing Buechner's great affection for *The Wizard of Oz*, what follows comes as another surprise. He describes this beloved story as a "fairy tale dehumbugged."[27] It is a secular fairy tale: the wizard is more therapist than magic man, helping the scarecrow, tin man, and cowardly lion see they had the brains, heart, and courage they needed inside themselves all along. The wizard bumbles with his hot air balloon, and before he can help Dorothy return home, he flies away. Glenda the good witch then appears and delivers a similar message to Dorothy: she had the power to get back to Kansas all along. The message is not "Joy beyond the walls of the world"; it is joy here and now through a can-do attitude and a little help from your friends.

After deconstructing *Oz* into a secular fairy tale, Buechner notes that the original book was published in 1900 and that it "foreshadows something of what became of the fairy tale of the Gospel in the century it ushered in."[28]

In the hands of the preachers of the modern day, the gospel, Buechner maintains, has become a similar humanist fairy tale. Today's preacher "secularizes and makes rational . . . adapts and makes relevant . . . demythologizes and makes credible."[29] We shrink the gospel to a smaller, controllable size:

> The wild and joyful promise of the Gospel is reduced to promises more easily kept. The peace that passeth all understanding is reduced to peace that anybody can understand. The faith that can move mountains and raise the dead becomes faith that can help make life bearable until death ends it. Eternal life becomes a metaphor for the way the good a man did lives after him.[30]

Passages like these lead me to claim Buechner's theological home is really among the Pentecostals. I hear echoes of the faith-healer Agnes Sanford, impressing on the recently ordained Buechner the image of Christ standing in ten thousand churches with his hands tied behind his back because nobody dares ask him for anything. Buechner—a product of incredibly sane and rational places like Lawrenceville, Princeton, and Exeter—speaking at incredibly sane and rational Yale, has a bit of the wild-eyed madman about him as he exhorts preachers to let the gospel loose.

·✦·

After deconstructing Oz, Buechner surprises again: almost everyone is familiar with *The Wizard of Oz* from the classic MGM movie. But L. Frank Baum wrote several other *Oz* stories, and the young Buechner read them all. As he revealed in *The Eyes of the Heart*, he still has his childhood *Oz* books in his Magic Kingdom. In those stories, Dorothy keeps returning to Oz because she is more alive there than in Kansas. The wizard, it turns out in the end, isn't a humbug after all; he really is a wonderful wizard, the great and powerful Oz. And we are like Dorothy. We keep returning because the deepest part of us, the child in us who believes fairy tales might be true after all, longs for our true home: Oz, Narnia, Middle Earth— all these places offer glimpses of heaven, our true home. We come to church for that glimpse. May all preachers tell the truth of the story too good not to be true.

SECRETS IN THE DARK:
THE WONDER OF WORDS

I ONCE HEARD A HIGHLY RESPECTED TEACHER of homiletics say that he would never tell students to imitate Buechner. "Their attempts to bare their souls would slip easily into narcissism," he said. "Few have the skills Buchner has to mine the depths of his life and speak about it with grace and dexterity."

While I agree with his aversion to narcissistic preaching, I think he has actually confused Buechner the memoirist for Buechner the preacher. Buechner doesn't spill his darkest secrets in his sermons. He talks about the biblical text much more than himself—Buechner has taken 2 Corinthians 4:5 to heart: "For we do not proclaim ourselves; we proclaim Jesus Christ as Lord." However, his sermons (like everything else he writes) rise from the crucible of the experiences that have formed him. There is a fine distinction here, the distinction between talking *about* your experience and talking *out of* your experience. Buechner told an interviewer,

> You don't have to use the "I" all the time to talk out of your
> own experience. Tillich never used "I" as far as I know, or very
> rarely, and yet there are times, even when speaking really quite

abstractly, where you know he's talking out of what happened to Paul Tillich. You can hear it, as a friend can hear it. . . . If you were just telling your own experience for the sake of drawing attention to yourself and let it end there, that would be anathema, that would be heresy, that would be some sort of ego trip. . . . You are drawing on your own experience, not to draw attention to yourself but to point towards that which you have experienced which is God and Christ moving in the world. Everything you say must be subordinated to that.[1]

·✦·

Secrets in the Dark is a "greatest hits" collection featuring fifty years of Buechner's sermons. Most of the material in the book was first published in *The Magnificent Defeat*, *The Hungering Dark*, *A Room Called Remember*, *The Clown in the Belfry*, and *The Longing for Home*. However, a handful of sermons are included that were developed after those books were published. And not every entry is a sermon. There are other addresses inside, including my favorite, "Adolescence and the Stewardship of Pain." What they all have in common is that they were first delivered orally, which is to say they were written for the ear instead of the eye.

I heard one of these sermons, "The Seeing Heart," in person. In 2004, Buechner preached at my church. It was a memorable morning—his appearance was tied in with Calvin College's Festival of Faith and Writing, and the church was full of visitors, including Barbara Brown Taylor. In the swarm of people after the service, someone stole the pulpit Bible Buechner had used. I have never been quite sure what to make of this bizarre development. Stealing a Bible from a church is like stealing shampoo from your hotel bathroom. They want you to have it.

·✦·

When Buechner was in seminary, he thought of writing novels and writing sermons as an either/or proposition. Eventually, he came to see all of his writing as ministry, but if he'd never come to that realization, he could have fashioned a fine career as a preacher. It's not a given that a novelist or memoirist will cross genres easily—I remember hearing a noted memoirist preach and being shocked at how below average the sermon turned out to be. Writing well in one genre doesn't mean you necessarily will write well in others.

I wish preachers were encouraged to imitate Buechner. I wish it so much that I will suggest four skills preachers might borrow from Buechner using examples from *Secrets in the Dark*.

TELL IT STRAIGHT

During Buechner's first years in ministry at Exeter, he knew he couldn't get away with serving up lukewarm Bible stories with a few religious clichés thrown in. Nothing less than authenticity would work with those students, and Buechner's book *Telling the Truth* took root there.

Telling it straight also means not assuming anything about the faith of one's listeners. Karl Barth's "Is it true?" question must have seemed emblazoned on the forehead of every young man who was required to fill the student church during Buechner's time at Exeter. He continually asks questions from a skeptical point of view and never assumes religious questions are settled; *if* is always the operative word.

He begins "The Message in the Stars" with the question, "If God really exists, why in heaven's name does God not prove that he exists instead of leaving us here in our terrible uncertainty?"[2] He knew his students wondered this and had the nerve to go ahead and ask it. By way of an answer, he plays with the idea of God rearranging a constellation of stars and spelling out "*I Really Exist*" in the night sky. He then speculates about how people might respond to that message. He imagines instant obedience followed by dwindling interest. As the sermon continues, Buechner points out that even though we all crave some sort of demonstrable proof of God's existence, that sort of proof isn't what we really need. We don't just want to know God exists; we want to know God is involved in "the fragrant muck and misery and marvel"[3] of our world and in our lives. It's God's presence that we're really after—we don't need God in the stars; we need God in our lives. It's a powerful message that starts with an honest question.

He is reluctant to offer answers before exploring questions. "Can it be true?" he asks, echoing Barth in a sermon called "Faith." "No, of course it cannot . . . how can it possibly be true?" This sort of honesty is disarming—it's the last thing we think a minister is supposed to say, and as a result it grabs our attention. "Yet how can it not be true when our own hearts bear such powerful witness to it, when blessed moments out of our own lives speak of it so eloquently?" As I have noted in previous chapters, this is how Buechner does apologetics—not drawing on reason or proof but experience. I find myself nodding in agreement with both sides of his argument. I agree that the Christian story sounds preposterous and unbelievable. Yet I also agree that there have been moments that convince me it has to be true. I agree with both sides at once—and then Buechner addresses my "in-betweenness" head on: "And that no-man's-land between the Yes and the No, that everyman's land, is where faith stands and has always stood."[4] Exactly! Note too the skill of his word choice. He flips "no-man's land" into "everyman's land," that universal space between yes and no that we all inhabit (even those who claim to have a lot of certainty one way or another). It is the space I live in every day, the space of "Lord, I believe; help my unbelief."

Buechner anticipates doubt and recognizes it as a normal part of faith. Noting that the scriptures called that famous doubter Thomas "the twin," Buechner says, "If you want to know who the other twin is, I can tell you. I am the other twin, and unless I miss my guess, so are you."[5]

This is honest—so honest that some have concluded Buechner doesn't have much faith and that he must be constantly waffling. However, when asked about his doubts directly, he told an interviewer,

> People talk about that—my doubts—and I have doubts about certain aspects of things and I certainly have doubts about the literal truth of some of the claims made for Jesus. Did he really come out of the tomb? Did he walk on the water? But they are doubts that don't bother me at all—I don't really care whether he did or not. . . . I think about that essay of John Updike's where he says God saves his deepest silence for the saints . . . I have never looked into the abyss and seen nothing. I've never had doubt that way. I've always had this sense that no matter how awful, that underneath are the everlasting arms, that the ending ultimately is a happy ending . . . I think there is blessing at the heart of it, holiness at the heart of it.[6]

Buechner addresses the same idea in *The Longing for Home*, making a distinction there between "mind doubt" and "stomach doubt." "I have never felt in my *stomach*," he writes, "what it must be to confront utter meaninglessness because far beneath all my misgivings, there is always the assumption that, beyond my power to understand, all is well."[7]

Buechner is not undecided about his faith. His doubts are similar to my doubts and most probably similar to yours as well. His commitment to honesty, to telling the truth, to telling it straight, prevents him from portraying his own faith in heroic, mountaintop terms and also prevents him from assuming anything about his listeners.

Tell It Real

"Show, don't tell," is common advice for writers. Don't say, "It was cold"; show us how cold it was. Don't say, "I was anxious"; show us your anxiety. Buechner applies this maxim to his sermons primarily by telling stories. And as I have said repeatedly, he often tells stories from his own experience.

His sermon "Two Narrow Words" provides a stunning example. He weaves Job's anguished "Oh, that I knew where I might find him" (Job 23:3) with Paul's similarly anguished "we were so utterly, unbearably crushed that we despaired of life itself" (2 Cor 1:8). To those texts he adds a quote from Sir Walter Raleigh that ends with the "two narrow words" *hic jacet*: "here lies." The sermon is spiked with intensity. Death, as Raleigh points out, is universal and inevitable. Life, as Job and Paul point out, is filled with darkness and pain. With trademark honesty, Buechner raises Job's question for all of us: "If God is all he's cracked up to be, then for God's sake, for Christ's sweet sake, where is he?"[8]

It's at this moment that Buechner surprises with an illustration drawn from his experience. He tells of the moment he met his first grandchild. Such an incident is ripe for sentimentalizing, but not in Buechner's hands. They met on a staircase:

> My daughter Dinah, his mother, was coming down carrying him in her arms, and I was going up with my heart in my mouth to meet him—this very small boy named Oliver with the blood in his veins of so many people I have loved, this fragile bit of a two-month-old child who, God willing, will carry some fragment of who I am into a future I will never see. He was on his way down into the world, and I was on my way up out of it. . . . On the one hand, there was my joy at seeing him for the first time, which brought tears to my eyes, but on

the other hand, part of where those tears came from was the realization that the world he was entering was full of great sorrow as well as of great gladness, the realization that he will one day die even as I also will one day die before I can ever know what becomes of him.[9]

The sermon gets brighter from there. (How could it not?) The anguish of Job and Paul is not the end of either of their stories; both experienced the presence of God in manifest ways and did not stay in the abyss. The sermon ends with the assurance that Job and Paul both found the light that shines in the darkness, and that light shines on us as well. However, the concrete example Buechner uses, of meeting his grandson on a staircase and seeing not only the possibility of his life but the reality of his death, is sobering.

A happier sermon, "The Great Dance," illustrates the difference between fleeting happiness and biblical joy using the beachside encounter of the risen Jesus with Peter recorded in John 21 as its text. Buechner begins the sermon with a story about going to Sea World with his wife and daughter and finding his eyes filling with tears watching the killer whale show because it reflected the delight and beauty of creation. When Buechner explained his reaction to his wife and daughter, they said that their eyes had filled with tears too. Years later, Buechner shared this story at a preaching seminar. After hearing the story, one of the participants approached Buechner with the text of a sermon he'd preached a few weeks earlier. In his sermon, that man told of going to Sea World and having his eyes fill with tears at the beauty of the great animals. "The world is full of darkness," Buechner says. "But what I think we caught sight of in that tourist trap in Orlando, Florida, of all places, was that at the heart of darkness—whoever would have believed it?—there is joy unimaginable."[10] He goes from there to retell the biblical story from

John 21—another story with water, fish, sun, sky, and most likely tears as well. Out of the darkness of the crucifixion comes the unimaginable joy of the resurrection, and when Jesus tells Peter to feed his sheep, Buechner imagines one of the things he means is that we are to tell each other our own stories of our encounters with the sort of unimaginable joy that brings tears into our eyes.

Stories like these—of meeting his grandson or seeing the show at Sea World—populate Buechner's sermons. They are riveting because they are real. In another sermon, he tells of driving into New York City on a splendid spring day and being overcome with the beauty of the city. After parking, he walked along Central Park South, and a woman going the other way said, "Jesus loves you" as he passed her. After that encounter, he felt as if the streets were paved with gold. "Nothing was different," he says. "Everything was different. The city was transfigured. I was transfigured. It was a new New York coming down out of heaven adorned like a bride prepared for her husband."[11] Buechner's sermons take abstract concepts like love, joy, and beauty and make them palpably real. In no way are the stories or sermons narcissistic. Buechner is not the hero in any of them, nor some sort of saint or spiritual giant. He is simply his human self, telling it real from his experience. By entering the story with him, we go to deep places—first we move further into the biblical text and then ultimately into the presence of God. He does not "proclaim himself" but draws on his experience and invites us through his words into deep and powerful mysteries.

Tell It Slant

Emily Dickinson's famous maxim applies here especially in the creativity Buechner displays retelling biblical stories. Just as preachers lose their listeners when they speak in abstractions, they also lose their listeners when they retell Bible stories in unimaginative language and parrot back a scriptural story that was just read a few moments earlier.

Buechner has repeatedly demonstrated his capacity to refresh and renew biblical characters and stories in books like *Peculiar Treasures* and *The Son of Laughter*, and with his memorable sketches of Pontius Pilate and Abraham and Sarah in *Telling the Truth*. He uses that same creative skill throughout the sermons in *Secrets in the Dark*.

The oldest sermon included in this volume is "The Magnificent Defeat," the title sermon from his first sermon collection. It opens with a description of Isaac on the day Jacob stole Esau's blessing. Buechner describes Isaac's head as "trembling under the weight of his great age, his eyes cobwebbed around with many wrinkles."[12] He doesn't just say, "Isaac was old"—he shows us Isaac. Buechner goes on to describe Jacob's all-night wrestling match at the river Jabbok and ends with the image of Jacob "limping home against the great conflagration of the dawn." He then draws a parallel to Jesus "staggering on broken feet out of the tomb toward the resurrection."[13] Instead of saying, "There is irony in both the stories of Jacob and Jesus because in each case defeat became victory," we have Jacob "limping home" and Jesus "staggering on broken feet." Images are created, and listeners' minds are engaged. He even uses the four-syllable word *conflagration* and gets away with it. You can't use a word like that often, but here it is used to great effect. "Great conflagration of the dawn" has a majestic quality that "morning sunrise" lacks. It gives a noble quality to Jacob.

Sometimes all a sermon needs to make it memorable is one phrase. In a sermon based on Isaiah's prophecy about the Messiah, Buechner says "all heaven broke loose"[14] on the night of Jesus' birth. It's a play on the phrase "all hell broke loose," originally from Milton's *Paradise*

Lost. By switching "heaven" for "hell," Buechner again engages our imaginations. Immediately we think of what heaven breaking loose might look like and see the shepherds, hear the angel choirs, imagine the wise men following the star, and think of the God of the universe as a child in a manger.

At Union Seminary, Buechner learned from James Muilenburg that we never really understand a Bible story until we understand it as our story. In one of the later sermons contained in *Secrets in the Dark*, "Jairus's Daughter," Buechner begins by building a bridge between Bible times and our time, insisting Bible stories are not "about stained-glass people at all but about people who lived and breathed and sweated and made love and used bad language when they tripped over furniture in the dark."[15]

He grabs our attention in that sermon by wondering how you might distinguish Jesus in a crowd and then asks if Jesus is the one who looks a little like Osama bin Laden. Jesus probably did look more like Osama bin Laden than the many familiar representations of him, where he looks more Western European than Middle Eastern.

Buechner asks questions repeatedly in this sermon. What would it have been like to be close to Jesus, so close that "he brushed against you so that for a second or two you actually felt the solid flesh and bone of him, smelled the smell of him?"[16] As the crowd moves, Jairus is told his daughter has died, and Jesus tells Jairus not to fear but to believe. "What is a man to believe when his whole life has blown up in his face?"[17] Buechner asks. That isn't just Jairus's question or Buechner's question. It's perhaps *the* question every one of us is most afraid to face. How does life make sense after the worst has happened?

The questions continue. When Jesus sees the girl's body, he says that she isn't dead but only sleeping. "Was he speaking literally?" Buechner asks. After Jesus raises the little girl, Buechner points out that the parents got their lives back in that moment as much as the little girl did, saying, "The worst thing that had ever happened to them had suddenly become the best thing that had ever happened to them."[18] He then asks more questions: What just happened? What kind of story is this? And why the command not to talk about it? It's a miracle, he says, that ends with a question mark instead of an exclamation point.

He closes by leading us into Muilenburg's challenge to see it as a story about ourselves. "Get up" is the message. Jesus is saying "Get up" to all of us, and he has "the power to give life not just to the dead like the child, but to those who are only partly alive, which is to say . . . people like you and me."[19] Almost the whole sermon is a retelling of the Bible story, but it is done in such a creative and imaginative way that we can't help but listen to it as if it's the first time we've heard it. Telling the old story in a new way is a skill worth imitating.

TELL IT SLOW

Buechner initially aspired to be a poet. His first professionally published piece was the poem "Fat Man's Prescription" in *Poetry* magazine in 1946. His last book, *The Yellow Leaves*, published sixty-two years later, concludes with a series of poems. Other books of his over the years occasionally included poems, or Buechner poems would pop up occasionally in magazines like *The Christian Century*, or even *Blair & Ketchum's Country Journal*, which published Buechner's poem "Follensby Pond" in 1983.

Buechner's musing about art in *Whistling in the Dark* makes the case that art puts a frame around ordinary things so that we will pay attention.[20] While painters use literal frames and writers use words, poets especially choose words carefully in order that we might slow down and take notice of what's right in front of us. There is a focus on sound, rhythm, and imagery that means poems aren't read (or written) in a hurry. Buechner chooses words carefully in all his writing, and his care with words is particularly evident in his sermons.

I've already cited several examples—like "fragrant muck and misery and marvel," "everyman's land," "staggering on broken feet," and "all heaven broke loose." A final example is found in *Secrets in the Dark*'s title sermon, "The Secret in the Dark." In it Buechner speaks of a tree he sees in Florida. On most days when wintering in Florida, he would take an early morning walk along the inland waterway. A particular tree marked the northernmost point on his walk where he would turn and head home. He describes the tree as having "multiple trunks all braided and buttressed, and roots that snake out over the ground as widely as its branches snake out into the air."[21]

I would wager that if you put a hundred people into a room and asked them to write down as many words as they could think of to describe a tree trunk, no one would come up with *braided* or *buttressed*. The tree is a tropical variety with multiple trunks, and *braided* is the perfect word to describe how those trunks fit together. *Buttressed* is an even more perfect word that describes how the trunks emerge from the center of the tree and hold it into the ground. *Snake* is another remarkable word choice in that sentence. Who would use that word to describe a tree? Buechner is showing that the tree is alive, moving, and writhing in its roots and branches.

Buechner goes on to say that he always stops to touch the tree with his hand or sometimes with his cheek, but that "on one particular morning I found myself touching it not to bless it for once, but to ask its blessing, so that I myself might move toward old age and death with something like its stunning grace and courage."[22] (Kenzie Maxwell has a very similar encounter with a very similar tree in Buechner's novel *The Storm*.)

If all Buechner had said was that he asked a tree for its blessing one day, we might question his sanity. But after giving such a picture of the tree, we feel its gravitas and respect its life, if not its wisdom. Buechner's actions in this light are normal, not eccentric or foolish.

What does any of this have to do with the message of the sermon? Buechner's text is the story of the disciples who encounter but don't recognize the risen Jesus on the Emmaus Road. "Their eyes were kept from recognizing him" is the way Luke puts it, and Buechner adds that their eyes remind him of his eyes, which tend to "see everything except what matters most."[23] It was only when Jesus broke bread with his followers that they recognized him, and Buechner's example of really seeing the old tree for what it was on one particular day out of the hundreds he looked at it parallels the experience of recognition the disciples had on the way to Emmaus. It's all set up by the word choices Buechner makes.

·✦·

Because I work at a seminary, I hear more sermons than a typical churchgoer—probably about two hundred a year. I often find myself wishing the preacher would take more time to do the four things I've mentioned in this chapter. I wish preachers would take more time to carefully choose words. I wish preachers would take the time to think creatively about the scriptural text. Too many preachers speak in abstractions instead of telling concrete stories, especially stories drawn from their own experience, and their sermons are poorer because of this. Regarding honesty, it is extremely rare for any of the preachers I hear to acknowledge either their listeners' doubts or their own doubts. I wish they did. I crave authenticity.

In contrast to the famous teacher of preaching I referenced at the beginning of the chapter, I believe there is much not only to learn but also to emulate from Frederick Buechner as a preacher. *Secrets in the Dark* belongs not only in the library of every preacher but in the library of anyone who cares about how the Christian faith is communicated. It is a book full of treasures, and our final Buechner essential.

READING
BUECHNER TODAY

F REDERICK BUECHNER AND HIS WIFE, Judy, still live in
Vermont. Their three daughters and extended family remain
close, and the grandchildren are now moving into adulthood.

It's been over ten years since the publication of *The Yellow Leaves*,
Buechner's last book of new material, and almost seven decades since
the publication of *A Long Day's Dying*. How now do we assess Buechner's career? What has he done well? Where has he fallen short? What
has been his influence? Will his writing endure and reach new generations of readers? Most important, what does Buechner have to say
to us today?

When considering his own career, the one regret I've heard
Buechner voice is that he never found a larger audience. No book of
Buechner's sold more than *A Long Day's Dying*. Speaking about that,
Buechner told Dale Brown,

> Certainly it was the most successful book I've ever written. It's
> sort of pathetic, because I wrote it when I was twenty-three
> years old or something like that. I don't think it plays much of
> a part anymore. I would certainly love to have more readers. I

would love to have a book as successful today as that book was then—not for the sake of fame or fortune so much as just for the sake of having more readers to share my thoughts with.[1]

I wonder if receiving the awards he came so close to—the Pulitzer Prize and National Book Award for Fiction—would have made a difference. Would "Winner of the Pulitzer Prize" have brought more readers than "Pulitzer Prize Nominee"?

I wonder too if Buechner would be better known had the attempts to bring the Bebb books and *Godric* to the screen succeeded. The rumor was that the actor Ned Beatty held the rights to Bebb and wanted to adapt it with himself in the lead role, and I have also heard that various treatments of *Godric* circulated in Hollywood. These things never came to fruition, and the wider audience never materialized.

Through the Buechner Center, Buechner's work is reaching a bigger audience on the internet, one or two paragraphs at a time. Thousands of readers subscribe to a daily word from Buechner (drawn from his many books), and Buechner even seems like an internet maven—I've had friends breathlessly tell me that Frederick Buechner "liked" something they posted on Facebook or Twitter. I hate to disappoint anyone, but that's the Buechner Center. Buechner is not spending his nineties in Vermont minding social media.

In addition to the online presence, the Buechner Center also has had a hand in the publication of the three additional Buechner titles (*Buechner 101*, *The Remarkable Ordinary*, and *A Crazy, Holy Grace*) published since *The Yellow Leaves*.

Although that wider audience eluded Buechner in his day, there is no question of Buechner's influence on many other significant writers. The list of authors who have identified as Buechner admirers is wide and varied, including John Irving, Maya Angelou, Anne Lamott, Annie Dillard, Philip Yancey, Barbara Brown Taylor, Russell

Moore, Eugene Peterson, Rob Bell, Madeleine L'Engle, and Lauren Winner as well as musicians Michael Card and Andrew Peterson. I appreciate both his influence on other artists and the robust internet presence. Although I believe people will be better served by reading the original books, a few paragraphs are better than nothing.

My strong conviction is we need Buechner's voice today more than ever. The one word that best describes both the church and our wider culture at the moment is *polarized*. To paraphrase William Butler Yeats, the center has not held, and there are constant forces that move everything toward one pole or the other. There is precious little middle ground anymore.

Buechner, however, refuses to be pushed toward a side. Attempts to classify him result in oxymorons. He is a conservative liberal. Or is he a liberal conservative? He is a Pentecostal mainliner, or is he a mainline Pentecostal? He is a novelist ordained to evangelize, and while that may not be an oxymoron, it is certainly unique. There are other ordained ministers who write novels, but none of them are being nominated for America's most prestigious literary awards. He is an ordained novelist who refuses to preach in his novels while being one of our greatest preachers. He is also a creative, wry, and witty theologian, which is certainly another oxymoron. I am in the very small number of people who can truthfully say, "Some of my best friends are theologians," and while they generally appreciate great literature, the abstract nature of their field limits its literary quality. Buechner wrote theology, but it was never abstract. It was always personal and highly pastoral.

I mentioned in the first chapter that our need for wise guides in our fragmented and complex world is one reason for the current popularity of memoirs. Buechner was a pioneer in the spiritual memoir movement, and we look to him still to help show the way. We need his voice to help affirm faith in a world that is falling apart.

What does it mean to believe in God when there is so much evidence to the contrary? This is Buechner's great theme and the thread that holds the novels, memoirs, popular theology, and sermons together.

The earliest novels explored the emptiness and despair of modern life without God. Beginning with the clack-clack of two branches in 1965 in *The Final Beast*, Buechner's novels assumed God was present, alive, and active, albeit "here and there, now and then, mostly hidden."[2]

Only those who are paying attention notice the subterranean presence of grace. It is, as Buechner says in *The Final Beast*, as subtle as "the approach of the approach perhaps of splendor."[3] As Buechner reached his most productive years, he settled on writing novels about saints, and Leo Bebb, Godric, Brendan, and Jacob—who resided on different continents in different centuries—were united by being saints with feet of clay, the only kind of saint Buechner knew. Yes, each saint was a lifegiver, but what matters most in their stories is the grace and love given to them, the sense that just below the surface is something—or Someone—working for good.

Eventually, as he began writing about his life, he wrote his memoirs like he wrote his novels, exhibiting his sense of the subterranean presence of grace. From there came *Wishful Thinking* and the other books of theology, *Telling the Truth*, and collections of sermons. The ABC books of theology and the sermons bear the same witness to God's subterranean presence.

Buechner reflected on the meaning of the "subterranean presence of grace," saying,

> That's a wonderful way to put it. It's beneath the surface; it's not right there like the brass band announcing itself, but it comes and it touches and it strikes in ways that always leave us free to either not even notice it or to draw back from it. . . . But that's what I try to do, to speak about human beings and the

rough-and-tumble of human existence, human beings who are here and there touched by grace through people they come to know or through things that happen to them or things that don't happen to them.[4]

·✦·

In his book *Soul Survivor,* the popular Christian author Philip Yancey writes thirteen profiles of the people who have had the largest influence on the development of his faith. Amid prominent figures such as Martin Luther King Jr. and Mahatma Gandhi, and formidable writers such as Leo Tolstoy, G. K. Chesterton, and John Donne, there is a chapter about Frederick Buechner. Yancey points to Buechner's ability to write about faith in fresh ways:

> Buechner became for me a mentor in rediscovering a gospel that had grown all too familiar. Unlike me, he did not have to unlearn what he had learned in church, since he had never learned much in church. His pilgrimage he undertook voluntarily as an adult, a journey fraught with risk and danger, not a group tour with a prearranged itinerary. As a result, he makes the basic facts of the gospel glow as though he has just discovered them in a pottery jar in the Middle East. The Christian faith strikes him as good news because it presents the truth of the world as he has experienced it, giving words to the deepest things he has felt by living on this planet.[5]

That ability to "make the basic facts of the gospel glow," or, as Yancey puts it later, tell the "old, old story in a new way,"[6] has its roots in Buechner's skill as a novelist. His eye for detail and nose for plot have served him well. Buechner's ability to speak of the "deepest things" makes his particular story universal. Although Buechner's particular story is unique, readers return, over and over, to Buechner (especially to the memoirs) because of what we discover about ourselves in them.

Yancey also says he "learned from Buechner the advantage of saying too little rather than too much,"[7] and Buechner's brevity should also be listed as one of his strengths. Six of the ten books I've identified as essentials barely break one hundred pages. The ability to use an economy of words while speaking of the deepest things is evidence of Buechner's mastery of his craft.

Another theme of Buechner's writing that remains as important today as when his books were first written is suicide. There are very few models of how to talk about suicide in healthy ways in our culture, the church, or most families. Suicide creates great shame and an endless number of unanswered questions. Buechner's books break the silence and get this taboo subject out in the open.

· ✦ ·

I do have a criticism as I reflect on Buechner's life and career. Belief is a personal matter, but it is also a corporate matter. Here Buechner falls short, and no assessment of his career from a faith-based point of view would be complete without noting this. His theology of the church pretty much begins and ends with the statement that the church should be more like Alcoholics Anonymous. He speaks of the church as a critic rather than as an active participant. With the exception of the days he was preaching, he rarely found himself in church on Sunday mornings and never really found a local expression of the church that he could be comfortable in. (The exception is St. Barnabas in Glen Ellyn, Illinois, which he attended while teaching at Wheaton.)

Buechner certainly is not alone in his lack of church affiliation. He foreshadowed current trends. There are a number of prominent religious voices that once led churches who have moved out. Buechner never moved out because he never moved in. He grew up outside the church, went to George Buttrick's church around the time of his conversion, attended seminary, became a school minister, and then moved to Vermont and never settled in a church. He never felt a calling to get inside and try to fix things. Here I draw an unfavorable comparison of Buechner to Marilynne Robinson. Both write exquisite novels and deep theological essays. But Robinson is invested in the life of a local congregation, and any critique she offers comes from the inside.

We live in a strange moment in the history of the church, when it seems very possible for an individual to profess his or her intimate relationship with Christ outside of a relationship with the body of Christ, the local church. I understand the many reasons why people wind up there. But that is not the historic Christian faith, the faith that is nurtured not in isolation but in community with others and the great cloud of witnesses who have gone before.

·✦·

In October 2017, at the time of the release of the "new" Buechner books *The Remarkable Ordinary* and *A Crazy, Holy Grace*, Russell Moore, a leader in the Southern Baptist Convention, wrote an appreciative article about Buechner in *Christianity Today*. He recounts his first exposure to Buechner and the realization that "this was someone who didn't seek to manipulate my emotions or enlist me in a cause. He just told the truth as he saw it." Later, Moore adds, "Buechner does not always say what I want him to say, but I never wonder if he's telling me anything less than what he believes to be the truth. In an era of kinetic marketing and spin—as much within the church as anywhere else—that alone is remarkable."[8]

It is that commitment to honesty that sets Buechner apart. Karl Barth's "Is it true?" question, which Buechner has imagined on the lips of every reader and listener since his days at Exeter, drove him. When he wrote his Beecher lectures for Yale, he was compelled to name them *Telling the Truth* because there is no more important task for preachers. It only takes thirteen pages in that book until Jesus' mute witness to the truth makes Pontius Pilate's head swim. Our heads swim, too, as Buechner winds his way, imploring and exhorting preachers to tell the truth about themselves and the gospel—the tragedy of it, the comedy of it, and the happily-ever-after fairy tale of it.

A friend made me smile once when he described a mutual acquaintance who struggled with integrity as a "genuine fake." Frederick Buechner is the opposite of that. There is a certain integrity to his work from *A Long Day's Dying* to *The Yellow Leaves*. As George Garrett said, "Touch any one thing in any one place and you are in touch with all of it," and "each new work seems to be what all the earlier work was all about."[9] There is a similar integrity between Buechner the man and Buechner the writer. He is the person who comes through on the page. This is also a gift in our particular cultural moment, when we've been shocked repeatedly by the private misbehavior of public figures not only in the celebrity world (where we've been preconditioned to expect such things) but in the church as well.

Buechner applies the same integrity and honesty when looking and listening to his own life. There is Naya (another lifegiver), the untimely and tragic suicide of his father, the magical sojourn to Bermuda, Lawrenceville, Jimmy Merrill, Princeton, Lawrenceville again, the unexpected early success quickly followed by failure, George Buttrick and Great Laughter, Union and James Muilenburg and Paul Tillich, Judy, Exeter, three daughters, settling in Vermont, wintering in Florida, anorexia, a license plate spelling *Trust*, and untold hours with a pad of unlined paper and a felt-tip pen in hand—not only bringing it all to life but seeing God in all of it, feeling the subterranean presence of grace, sensing that even in the most ordinary moments, God is speaking. The ordinary is revealed to be extraordinary because there are no ordinary moments, after all.

When all the layers are peeled away, there is joy at the heart of it—joy beyond the walls of the world and a love that will not let us go. Frederick Buechner has paid attention and told the truth, and our lives and our world are richer because of him.

EPILOGUE

T HE QUESTION I AM ASKED MOST about Frederick Buechner is, "Do you know him?" Not really, but we have had a couple of interesting encounters.

In 2004, Buechner was one of the headliners at Calvin College's Festival of Faith and Writing. Dale Brown, the conference organizer, invited me to be on the panel of a session called "Frederick Buechner: An Appreciation" the day before Buechner's keynote speech.

"I don't have the academic credentials," I protested. Dale didn't care. He asked if I might tell my story about my wife, Gretchen's, stroke and the healing I found when I read Buechner's essay on the stewardship of pain.

There were two others on the panel: Dr. James Cook, a beloved former professor of mine at Western Theological Seminary, and Dr. Leland Ryken, a distinguished professor of English and Buechner friend from Wheaton College. Roy Anker, a professor of English at Calvin, was the moderator. I felt extraordinarily nervous.

I got more nervous when the unexpected happened.

Roy Anker was introducing our panel when I saw the back doors of the auditorium open, and Fred and Judy Buechner walked in. I couldn't stop thinking, *Holy smokes, Frederick Buechner is going to listen to me talk about* him.

When my turn came, I poured my heart out with all the emotion and human feeling I had in me. I told my story as best I could and got emotional while I told it. When I finished, my old professor Jim Cook beamed at me like Wilbur must have looked at Orville when their plane took to the air. It was over in an instant, but it had gone better than I had allowed myself to imagine it could. Jim Cook and Leland Ryker followed me, and both gave stirring tributes. The audience was appreciative. My hopes for how Buechner would then respond were modest—maybe a hug followed by an invitation to drinks and dinner.

After Dr. Ryken finished, Roy Anker asked if there were any questions, and the first person who spoke said something like, "I never heard of this Bee-you-chner before—how come I've never heard of him?" To my disappointment, Fred and Judy stood up and exited the room as quietly as they had entered.

As they escaped down the hall, Jim Cook leaned over and whispered, "We don't possess the man, but we have his books."

I was deflated. Where was my hug? My dinner invitation?

I wanted contact. As I mentioned in chapter ten, he preached at my church two days later (the day someone stole the pulpit Bible). There was such a crush of people around him, I didn't get a chance to speak to him then either. So I wrote him a letter.

I don't remember exactly what I said, but I know I didn't say entirely what I felt like saying, which would have been, "How come you walked out on me?" Instead, I tried to say something self-deprecating about making a fool of myself because of the tears I had shed telling my story.

This was back in 2004, when people wrote letters by hand and sent them in envelopes using postage stamps. A few weeks later there was a small envelope with a Vermont postmark and "Buechner" stamped in the upper left corner in my mailbox. Inside was a letter written with a felt-tipped pen on an unlined piece of paper (just like his manuscripts).

The letter was beautiful and spare, and it included words such as "vividly" and "feelingly." Buechner wrote that he remembered my story about Gretchen's stroke very well, and that it had been great to hear not only my story but also the appreciation each of the speakers offered that day. Then he said that he and Judy had "scuttled out" because he didn't know how to handle our admiration. He thanked me for my kindness and offered me a blessing.

The letter was so elegant that on one level I didn't care what it said. He had answered me, and I was happy. And there was more to this than just a simple answer. He'd let me in to a place where he felt awkward and vulnerable. Being a "celebrity Christian" must be strange, and being the keynote speaker for Calvin's Festival put a spotlight on Buechner that made him uncomfortable. All that made sense to me, but over the years I've come to think there might have been even more going on.

Several years earlier, my brother had found a first edition of a book I was enamored with and gotten it signed by the author. I wrote that author and thanked him for signing my book and then asked him about thirty-eight thousand questions. He wrote back and said, "As to all your questions, I don't know any answers anymore." Those words were written on top of a copy of his bibliography. It took a while, but I eventually realized he was telling me that everything he had to say was in his books.

Jim Cook had said as much about Buechner in the sentence, "We don't possess the man, but we have his books." Regardless of my ridiculous fan-boy expectations, Buechner had already given me (and all the rest of us) the pieces of himself we most needed through his books.

Still, I wanted more.

•✦•

I had another chance a few years later. My friend Dale Brown, who had organized Buechner's appearance at Calvin, had moved from there to King College in Tennessee and invited me to participate in the opening of the Buechner Institute he'd established. The participants were being treated to breakfast before the program began. Since I didn't really know anybody (I had heard of almost all of them but didn't know them), I sat down alone at a table with some quiche and a couple of sausage links for company. A few moments later the renowned Old Testament scholar Walter Brueggemann sat down a couple of chairs away from me. I was in the process of saying something witty like, "Hello, Walter Brueggemann," when I felt someone else behind us. Sure enough, it was Frederick Buechner. He took the empty chair between Walter Brueggemann and me. I immediately choked on a sausage while Buechner and Brueggemann began chatting. I then nibbled at my quiche, feeling like one of the disciples on the Mount of Transfiguration gazing at Moses and Elijah. After a couple of minutes, Buechner got up and went to greet someone he recognized at another table. Brueggemann then faced me, and I think I impressed him with a quick, "Hello again, Walter Brueggemann."

My turn to talk with Buechner came after lunch. Fred and Judy had finished eating and were alone at a table. I walked over, introduced myself, and spewed forth something inane about how much he meant to me. He was warm, kind, and very gracious. I know so many stories about people meeting their heroes and finding out they are self-absorbed jerks. That didn't happen. Buechner was kind and affirming.

I do feel like I know Frederick Buechner, not because of those fleeting moments, but because of his books. I probably know more about his secrets and interior life than many of my real, in-person friends. "We don't possess the man," my wise old professor said, "but we have his books."

What gifts they are.

ACKNOWLEDGMENTS

A T THE INVITATION OF THE IRREPRESSIBLE BRIAN ALLAIN, I
presented a seminar about Frederick Buechner at Princeton
Theological Seminary in May 2017. Jeff Crosby, the guiding force at
IVP, was among those gathered that day, and after my presentation
he suggested I turn what I'd just done into a book proposal. That big
compliment subsequently created anxiety. How would I approach it?
The always amazing Jennifer Holberg helped me get a handle on the
project when she suggested I focus on my top ten essential Buechner
books. After the proposal was accepted, the wise-beyond-his-years
Ethan McCarthy of IVP shepherded the project to completion.

Isaac Anderson, a fantastic friend and writer, gave me much
helpful feedback as I started writing. Roger Nelson and Mark Hiskes,
Buechner lovers with keen intellects, read drafts of the manuscript
and were great sounding boards.

I spend my days in a wonderful community of faith and learning
at Western Theological Seminary, and members of our community
have provided valuable help. Tom Boogaart helped me with the
Jacob stories, Han-luen Kantzer Komline and Suzanne McDonald
both helped me with divine sovereignty and human freedom, and
David Stubbs helped me get a better (yet still tenuous) grasp on the

theology of Paul Tillich. While everyone at Western has been encouraging, no one has been more encouraging than Tim Brown. If you think you know the most encouraging person in the world and haven't met Tim, then you don't know the most encouraging person in the world. Also, I want to especially acknowledge the friendship and enthusiasm of Chuck DeGroat, Kyle Small, and Ben Connor. Each is a terrific teacher and scholar, and their care and interest in me, and this project, have helped a great deal.

My deep sadness while doing this book is that I couldn't talk to Dale Brown about it. Dale was for many years the animating force behind Calvin College's Festival of Faith and Writing and then started the Buechner Institute at King College. I turned often to Dale's *Book of Buechner* while doing my work, but I wish I could have spoken directly to my longtime friend. Dale and I bonded deeply over Buechner, and through Dale I had a number of tremendous Buechner experiences. Dale's untimely death has left a void in my life and the lives of many others.

Finally, although I am pretty sure that my seriously righteous friends Lori and Marty (the Balm in Gilead) DeHaan will think Buechner's theology is too lukewarm, I hope they like this book about him anyway.

Appendix

AN ANNOTATED BIBLIOGRAPHY
OF FREDERICK BUECHNER'S BOOKS

A LONG DAY'S DYING. NEW YORK: ALFRED A. KNOPF, 1950.

Novel—Tristram Bone is in love, but neither Bone nor any of the book's characters have the ability to speak clearly to each other. They speak about as clearly as Buechner's labored prose:

> She had not seen him for several months, and though this fact had not heretofore troubled her or him either, if his occasional letters were just evidence, she nevertheless discovered in herself now what she was pleased to imagine a long-standing desire to perform this possibly neglected division of her maternal duty.[1]

The style reflects the modernist literary scene of 1950. Today's reader looks for the seeds not only of the writer Buechner will become but also the religious topics he'll explore, and there are hints of what is coming. The first sentence says, "The mirror reflected what seemed at first a priest."[2] It isn't a priest; it is Bone, in a barber's cape and towel. Although Bone is celibate and detached like a priest, no one makes their confession to him; they lie and tell half-truths instead.

Ultimately, *A Long Day's Dying* is about alienation and estrangement. In theological terms, it is about sin. The origin of the book's title—Milton's *Paradise Lost*—provides a clue: like Adam and

Eve, the characters in *A Long Day's Dying* have been expelled from Eden's garden. There is no redemption waiting, and God is notable by his absence. Buechner had grown up among the leisured class in the places this book is set and found their lives meaningless and empty. His novel exposing that truth brought him literary recognition and notoriety, which he also found empty. He knew there must be more, and clearer visions and clearer writing lie ahead.

THE SEASONS' DIFFERENCE. NEW YORK: ALFRED A. KNOPF, 1952. **Novel**—There's a "Who are these people?" moment toward the end of *The Seasons' Difference*, where one of the characters notes that the others "had everything and nothing too."[3] Buechner is among the leisured elite again and doesn't like the characters. Nor, in retrospect, does he like the novel—it is perhaps his least favorite. The book is the rare Buechner title that has never been reissued, and I don't blame anyone for not making the effort to locate a copy to read.

And yet . . . and yet . . . for the Buechner aficionado, *The Seasons' Difference* is revelatory. Here is Buechner, a year *before* his conversion, writing about what it means to have faith: clearly the themes he is exploring are steps along his "sacred journey." A young man has had a religious vision and struggles to share it convincingly. He thinks if he can bring his small group of friends to just the right place at just the right time the vision might be repeated. A group of children stage a re-creation of the vision that momentarily confuses everyone. Did something actually happen? It did and it didn't. As the confusion is processed, the main character asserts we've already had enough shown to us: "The words and the example of Christ."[4]

One other reason for Buechnerphiles not to miss *The Seasons' Difference:* two teenaged characters are aspiring poets who call themselves "the Uglies," just like Buechner and Jimmy Merrill. The book is dedicated to "J.I.M."—James Ingram Merrill.

The Seasons' Difference is notable more for what it tells us about Buechner than for its merits as a novel. We're a long way from *Godric*, *Brendan*, or Leo Bebb, but we're on the way.

THE RETURN OF ANSEL GIBBS. NEW YORK: ALFRED A. KNOPF, 1958.

Novel—In January 1956, George P. Winship, Jr. published an article in *The Christian Century* discussing the state of religion in literature. After briefly reviewing the landscape, Winship said that he wished "more novelists would reflect deeply upon the questions that theologians study with special competence." Then, with his tongue planted in his cheek, he proposed that someone "catch a novelist and send him to a seminary."[5] Winship had no idea his fanciful suggestion had already happened. At the time his article was published, Frederick Buechner, a student at Union Theological Seminary, was writing his third novel, *The Return of Ansel Gibbs*.

Buechner has dropped the modernist style and, as a result, *Ansel Gibbs* is more accessible than its predecessors. The story revolves around politics—Ansel Gibbs's appointment to the president's cabinet is torpedoed by a blowhard populist senator who appeals to God and country.

There are easily identifiable autobiographical elements in the book—some of Paul Tillich's philosophy is espoused by Gibbs, and the character Henry Kuykendall is clearly James Muilenburg. Another autobiographical inclusion caused great pain: Buechner appropriated his father's suicide all the way down to the note left in the back pages of *Gone With the Wind* and created a visceral reaction from his mother, who felt betrayed.

The Return of Ansel Gibbs became a *Playhouse 90* feature on CBS with two-time Oscar winner Melvyn Douglas in the lead role. The book also won the Rosenthal award, which Buechner remembers best because Truman Capote brought Marilyn Monroe to the award dinner. The book marks another interesting step in Buechner's development.

THE FINAL BEAST. NEW YORK: ATHENEUM, 1965.

Novel—There are numerous autobiographical parallels between Theodore Nicolet, the young minister at the heart of *The Final Beast*, and his creator, Frederick Buechner. Both are the fathers of young daughters. Nicolet was converted listening to a minister preaching about Jesus being crowned amid confession and tears and great laughter. His grandfather's life story is a carbon copy of Buechner's great-grandfather's life story. He prays for a sign and hears two apple tree branches clack-clack, as Buechner did. He meets a faith healer who teaches him the same things about prayer the faith healer Agnes Sanford taught Buechner. A parishioner describes living in Bermuda in similar words to Buechner's in *The Sacred Journey*.

Although details come from Buechner's life, this story is pure novel, and it marks a significant turn in Buechner's career. It is his first attempt to write a novel where grace has the final say. The prejudicial critical reaction to a God-affirming book caught Buechner by surprise and marked him deeply.

Eugene Peterson's short tribute to the book captures well much of what there is to like about *The Final Beast*:

> When I became a pastor I supposed that the vocation would protect and nurture my spirituality—that since I was about the business of Scripture and prayer all day long, my whole Christian life would be easier. It didn't turn out that way. This novel is an account of how it did in fact turn out. The details and names in the story of this pastor are different, but the intricacies of temptation, the even greater intricacies of grace, and the infinite spiritualties of holiness are the same.[6]

THE MAGNIFICENT DEFEAT. NEW YORK: SEABURY, 1966.

Preaching—This is Buechner's first venture into nonfiction, a collection of eighteen sermons initially preached at Exeter. The theological convictions worked out in these pages would stick with Buechner for the remainder of his career. The story of Jacob is at the forefront, in the title sermon. A sermon on prayer has clearly been influenced by Agnes Sanford. In the introductory note, Buechner also acknowledges his debt to George Buttrick, as well as John Knox and Paul Scherer of Union. Knox was professor of sacred literature, and Scherer held the homiletics chair in Buechner's time. The other Union figure acknowledged is James Muilenburg, to whom the book is dedicated.

To understand Buechner as preacher, start with this book, and enjoy his highly literate and poetic narrative style.

THE HUNGERING DARK. NEW YORK: SEABURY, 1969.

Preaching—A follow-up to *The Magnificent Defeat*, this book is laid out in a similar fashion by the same publisher. This time there are thirteen sermons, most of which were first preached at Exeter. Ideas that will become Buechner trademarks are germinating; for example, in the sermon "The Calling of Voices," Buechner says, "We should go with our lives where we most need to go and where we are most needed."[7] It isn't too far from there to, "The place God calls you to is the place where your deep gladness and the world's deep hunger meet."[8] Another sermon, "A Sprig of Hope," is the best Noah's Ark sermon I can recall, with an explanation of why we turn the horrors of the flood into a story for children: "so that we can laugh instead of weep."[9] Unlike *The Magnificent Defeat*, this volume includes Buechner's beautiful prayers that follow each sermon, filled with his poetic language and longing heart.

THE ENTRANCE TO PORLOCK. NEW YORK: ATHENEUM, 1970.

Novel—This occupies the basement space along with *The Seasons' Difference* as Buechner's least favorite work. It's loosely based on the *Wizard of Oz*. A man, his two sons, and a grandson travel up a mountain to visit a wise man. The grandson is a sort of Dorothy figure, and his father, uncle, and grandfather need courage, heart, and brains. Their destination is a sanatorium for people with profound cognitive disabilities. Sad to say, the patients are caricatures rather than characters, and their treatment feels today like a wince-inducing misstep.

Most notable about this book is a scene toward the end, where the main character is doing a mind-reading trick for the assembled patients. He actually enters the mind of a young man and sees "a dead man lying on his back in the grass while two women in bathrobes worked his legs up and down like pump handles and the flattened face of a child watched from an upstairs window."[10] This is a description of the scene immediately following the discovery of Buechner's father's body—Buechner's mother and grandmother tried to revive him, and ten-year-old Buechner watched from above. As in *Ansel Gibbs*, Buechner is telling the secret of his father's suicide in an indirect manner.

The Entrance to Porlock is recommended reading only for deeply committed Buechnerphiles.

THE ALPHABET OF GRACE. NEW YORK: SEABURY, 1970.

Memoir—Originally delivered as the Noble Lectures at Harvard, as a memoir *The Alphabet of Grace* is thin—it describes one unremarkable day in Buechner's life in the fall of 1969. In other ways it is rich: he comes closer to writing directly about his father's suicide than in previous work; he raises his grandmother Naya from the dead for a conversation (the same trick he will employ twenty-nine years later in *The Eyes of the Heart*); and he describes his conversion and the events leading up to it in great detail, foreshadowing *The Sacred Journey*.

This is Buechner's first use of himself as his subject; in many ways, from this point on, his career will be defined by using his interior life as his theme. *The Alphabet of Grace* is where he first breaks the "listen to your life" ground so familiar to Buechner readers. He listens for God in the humdrum ordinariness of a day as he eats breakfast, takes his children to school, travels to the church where he writes, and works on refining a scene in his novel *The Entrance to Porlock*. God is working, and God is speaking, even in such an ordinary day as this.

The Alphabet of Grace also marks a new phase for Buechner's readers. Over the coming decades, he will publish nonfiction at a greater pace than fiction, giving readers not only the novels, where ideas are embedded in plots and characters, but also the accompanying nonfiction, where mysteries are spoken in straightforward language. The fiction and nonfiction offer different angles into the same place: the heart and mind of a deep thinker and gifted writer.

LION COUNTRY. NEW YORK: ATHENEUM, 1971.

Novel—There is an enormous distance in style between this book and the books that preceded it. Buechner relaxed, let his sense of humor out to play, and found his voice. He loves Leo Bebb, the round, bald, ex-con Bible salesman–turned-religious-diploma-mill operator with a droopy eyelid, calling him "strong in most of the places where I was weak, and mad as a hatter in most of the places where I was all too sane."[11] Part of finding his voice came from switching to first-person narration. The Bebb books are narrated by Antonio Parr, who answers a magazine article to *"Put yourself on God's payroll—go to work for Jesus now"* through Bible courses and

ordination offered by the Gospel Faith College from the Church of
Holy Love, Inc., in Armadillo, Florida.

Who is Bebb? A con man? A type of saint? A miracle worker? He
has spent five years in prison on a charge of exposing himself to a
group of children. (Or was he framed?) Parr travels to Florida to
expose Bebb, but of course it is Parr who winds up being exposed.
Florida is "lion country," where all sorts of wild things happen (including a romance that leads to marriage between Parr and Bebb's
daughter, Sharon), but no cat is wilder than big Leo.

The book was critically acclaimed and nominated for the National
Book Award. The world of Leo Bebb is just a little too out there for
me to name this as an essential, but anyone interested in diving fully
into Buechner should read it.

OPEN HEART. NEW YORK: ATHENEUM, 1972.

Novel—*Open Heart* is the most compelling of the Bebb novels. It's
also the saddest. Antonio Parr and Bebb's daughter, Sharon, have
moved to Connecticut, and their marriage is cracking. Bebb's guilt-
ridden, long-suffering, alcoholic wife, Lucille, commits suicide while
rocking in her chair, slitting her wrists as Scripture is read to her.
Over and over, the book is gospel as tragedy. "Sin is life wasted,"[12]
Bebb tells Antonio, and waste and decay are everywhere.

The book also features one of Buechner's best scenes. Antonio is
teaching the Buechner standby *King Lear*, and in the middle of an
average day, while a gym class does calisthenics outside and a bum-
blebee bangs into a chalkboard, something transcendent happens.
The class is made up of ordinary kids: a pimply boy, a fat boy, a dis-
interested jock, a beautiful girl in the fullness of her time. They are
considering Lear's line about "the poor naked wretches . . . that bide
the pelting of this pitiless storm." The fat boy suggests Lear is getting

kinder, and the girl thinks these words might even be a prayer. "Who are these poor naked wretches he's praying for, if she's right that he's praying?" Antonio asks. "We are," the pimply boy says in an attempt to be funny. No one laughs because the "unintended truth" of his words comes through. "They were the poor naked wretches and at least for a moment they knew they were."[13] As a reader, you pause, set the book down, and contemplate what has just happened.

Open Heart is tamer than *Lion Country*, but the Bebb books will venture into wilder territory from here. Before that happens, the pitiless storm rages on, and we are pelted—poor, naked wretches one and all.

WISHFUL THINKING: A THEOLOGICAL ABC. NEW YORK: HARPER & ROW, 1973.

Popular Theology—See chapter seven. Revised and expanded as *Wishful Thinking: A Seeker's ABC*. **San Francisco: HarperOne, 1993.**

LOVE FEAST. NEW YORK: ATHENEUM, 1974.

Novel—If *Open Heart* is the gospel as tragedy, *Love Feast* is tragedy deeper still. Everything falls apart. Antonio and Sharon separate, and Bebb is hounded by, among others, the IRS and an insurance investigator. Bebb, however, is mostly in the background here, as is Sharon. The focus of the series shifts to Antonio, and in the words of one reviewer, "He is suddenly asked to become a full-fledged human being, which is a terrible fate for someone born to be a comic seeing eye."[14] The pages without Sharon or Bebb (of which there are many) miss their sizzle and spark.

Antonio introduces the word *decathexis*, a stage in the death process where the dying person emotionally lets go of life. What death is he referring to? His own? His marriage's? Gradually we realize at least one *decathexis* in the novel is happening to Bebb, who goes into hiding and then orchestrates a reunion of Antonio and Sharon to say his goodbyes. He tells them, "Up's the only place I got left."[15] Instead of ascending into heaven in a golden chariot of fire, he goes in a fireball in an airplane piloted by his former cellmate, the arsonist "Fats" Golden. Their plane bursts into flame, and although no human remains are found at the crash site, witnesses attest they saw no one parachute out.

Buechner had written three Bebb books in four years, and there are enough endings in *Love Feast* to believe the curtain was coming down. But even from the grave Bebb won't let Buechner go, and three years later Bebb will be resurrected (sort of) in *Treasure Hunt*, the final volume of the tetralogy.

THE FACES OF JESUS. NEW YORK: RIVERDALE, 1974.

Popular Theology—Buechner wrote reflections on 150 different artistic representations of Jesus in this coffee table–sized book. It is among the least-known Buechner titles, maybe because of its unusual size—or maybe because Buechner wrote it in response to a publisher's request, meaning it didn't arise from the depths of his soul in the way his other books did. As Buechner might say, it wasn't written in blood.

The size problem was addressed with the book's rerelease in 2005 as *The Faces of Jesus: A Life Story.* Not only was the size shrunk, but the artwork was eliminated also, and Buechner's text (especially when he referred to the various pieces of art) was shortened. As a result, a 250-page oversized book became a hundred-page typically sized book. **Reissued as *The Faces of Jesus: A Life Story.* Brewster, MA: Paraclete, 2005.**

TELLING THE TRUTH: THE GOSPEL AS COMEDY, TRAGEDY, AND FAIRY TALE. SAN FRANCISCO: HARPER & ROW, 1977.

Preaching—See chapter nine.

TREASURE HUNT. NEW YORK: ATHENEUM, 1977.

Novel—The first *Star Wars* movie and *Close Encounters of the Third Kind* were both released in 1977, and Buechner did his own flying into outer space that year with *Treasure Hunt.* The book is the wildest installment in a wild series, yet like the others, it explores deep questions about faith.

How do you write a Bebb book after killing Leo Bebb? Bebb's voice is heard on cassette tapes of his sermons, letters are discovered that allow him to speak from the grave, and also a new character is introduced: "Babe" Bebb, Leo's twin brother. Babe is a "UFOlogist" who has transistors implanted in his teeth for extraterrestrial contact, proclaims Jesus was a spaceman, goes on nocturnal destructive rampages dressed as his wife, and is said to be just like Bebb "with the gospel left out."[16]

Amid the odd story and odder characters are strong passages about belief. Late in the book, Antonio makes his confession: "I had moved step by step to a kind of panicky openness to almost any possibility, which I suspect must be, if not the same thing as what people like Bebb would call faith, at least its kissing cousin."[17]

As the tetralogy closes, Sharon and Antonio return home to Connecticut, and the trees are covered with yellow ribbons and a sign that says, "Welcome Hone." "Hone" gets it right—we never quite can make it all the way home. Home is what we long for, but "hone" is the best we get. Home is the Eden we've been exiled from, the heaven we await, and the God we long to know, but this side of paradise, and certainly in the Bebb series, home is known more by its absence than presence.

PECULIAR TREASURES: A BIBLICAL WHO'S WHO.
SAN FRANCISCO: HARPER & ROW, 1979.
Popular Theology—See chapter eight.

THE BOOK OF BEBB. NEW YORK: ATHENEUM, 1979.
Novel—Because Buechner did some rewriting in order for the Bebb novels to be published together as a single volume, *The Book of Bebb* stands as a unique book.

Many Christian readers simply don't know what to make of the tetralogy, which both delights and frustrates. *Bebb* is far from the uplifting and inspirational fare many religious readers expect.

The Bebb series is not ultimately about the wild characters or the wild things they do. As Buechner wrote in the introduction to *The Book of Bebb*, "There is the sense of what the old hymn quaveringly addresses as 'O love that will not let me go,' the sense of an ultimate depth to things that is not finally indifferent as to whether people sink or swim but endlessly if always hiddenly refuses to abandon them."[18] God's grace is not about who we are; it's about who God is. The characters are drawn large so we might get a glimpse of what God is up to.

GODRIC. NEW YORK: ATHENEUM, 1980.
Novel—See chapter five.

THE SACRED JOURNEY. SAN FRANCISCO: HARPER & ROW, 1982.
Memoir—See chapter one.

NOW AND THEN. SAN FRANCISCO: HARPER & ROW, 1983.
Memoir—See chapter two.

A Room Called Remember: Uncollected Pieces.
San Francisco: Harper & Row, 1984.

Preaching—In the preface to *A Room Called Remember*, Buechner calls the book "a grab bag," which is correct. Fourteen of the eighteen entries are presented as sermons, but there are all sorts of pieces inside, including two *New York Times Book Review* essays on faith and literature; a seminary commencement address; a message at a different seminary on the speaking and writing of words; a memoir piece that first appeared in *The Christian Century*; and another piece that was featured in *Christianity Today.*

The opening sermon illustrates well Buechner's admonition that sermons should come from the depths instead of the shallows of the preacher's life. He relates a dream of a wonderful lost hotel room and is told in the dream all he needs to do to get the room again is ask for it by name: "Remember." Remembering is often fraught with guilt and shame, but coming to peace with our memories is where well-being, healing, and ultimately our true home lie. It is a powerful message that echoes what Buechner has modeled throughout his memoirs.

While the grab-bag nature of *A Room Called Remember* makes the whole a bit less than the sum of its parts, many of the parts are infused with enough wisdom, wonder, and love to make this book a welcome addition in any Buechner fan's library.

Brendan. New York: Atheneum, 1987.

Novel—If I were choosing fifteen Buechner essentials instead of ten, *Brendan* would make the list. As with *Godric*, Buechner has taken the story of a little-known saint and created a full life for him. Brendan was one of Ireland's early Christians and had significant adventures as a sailor—perhaps going as far as Newfoundland and Florida—in search of Tir-na-n-Og, a celestial paradise thought to exist beyond the western horizon. Because the book is set in the sixth century, when the new religion of Christianity was beginning to flourish in the midst of the Druid world, there is plenty of magic and myth in the story.

Brendan's companion, Finn, who serves as the narrator, provides the book's tension. Finn stands in for us, almost always leaving a question mark in place during Brendan's fantastic adventures. Brendan is a true believer, continually moving forward, while Finn stands to the side, sometimes marveling but often offering alternative explanations. Over time Brendan's enthusiastic faith wanes. The more venerated he becomes, the more he is filled with doubt and depression. He becomes less "saintly" and more human—and more likable as well. Because of that, *Brendan* is a book that takes a while to warm up to. The last hundred pages or so are especially gripping.

Brendan won the Belles-Lettres prize from the Conference on Christianity and Literature. The award is appropriate because *Brendan* is beautifully written in Buechner's trademark poetic prose.

WHISTLING IN THE DARK: AN ABC THEOLOGIZED.
SAN FRANCISCO: HARPER & ROW, 1988.

Popular Theology—With pen-and-ink illustrations from Katherine Buechner and the same alphabetical format, *Whistling in the Dark* forms a trilogy with *Wishful Thinking* and *Peculiar Treasures*. In this book, Buechner says he defines "just plain words," but those who have journeyed with Buechner know that there is nothing plain about word choices like "Anorexia," "Suicide," or "Alcoholics Anonymous."

The book doesn't quite rise to the level of its predecessors, perhaps because Buechner ranges a bit too far afield from theology and the Bible with entries like "Jogging," "Government," and "Patriotism."

Most of the entries, though, strike home with Buechner's usual wit and wisdom. Two of my favorites, "Algebraic Preaching" and "Tourist Preaching," make similar points about the same subject. "Algebraic Preaching" is using formulas like "accept Jesus Christ as your personal Lord and Savior and be saved from your sins," which makes as much sense as saying $x + y = z$. We don't know what the equation means without defining the variables. What do "sin," "salvation," "Jesus Christ," and "accept" mean? Similarly, "Tourist Preaching" equates preachers to Americans visiting a foreign country who think their English can be understood if they just speak louder and slower. Preachers have to translate biblical truths into language their hearers understand. This has been Buechner's mission from the first sentence of these lexical books. Rereleased as *Whistling in the Dark: A Doubter's Dictionary.* San Francisco: HarperSanFrancisco, 1993.

THE WIZARD'S TIDE. SAN FRANCISCO: HARPER & ROW, 1990.

Novel—Because *The Wizard's Tide* is a fictionalized version of events during Buechner's childhood, a strong argument can be made that it should be classified as a memoir instead of a novel. For example, in *The Book of Buechner*, Dale Brown lands on the side of memoir. Buechner published it as a novel, so I'm sticking with him, although it's fairly easy to see who's who. The Buechners become the Schroeders, Freddy becomes Teddy, Naya becomes Dan, and younger brother, Jamie, is a girl named Bean.

The book was imagined as a novel for young adults, but several publishers rejected it because of the "adult" themes, namely the family's dysfunction and ultimately Ted Schroeder's suicide. (In this telling he jumped in front of a subway train instead of starting the car in the family garage.)

It remains a very readable, hauntingly sad story that ends with notes of hope and signifies a key part of Buechner's inner work in the late 1980s. It truly is fiction because in this version Teddy resolves not to pretend as if his father didn't exist, and when his sister asks about the holy tide of Christmas mentioned in the song "God Rest Ye Merry Gentlemen," they decide it is a high tide, like the Wizard of Oz tide, the sort of tide capable of bringing everyone home, even their father. Although I don't count it as an essential, *The Wizard's Tide* is a beautiful story well worth reading.

TELLING SECRETS. SAN FRANCISCO: HARPERSANFRANCISCO, **1991.**

Memoir—See chapter three.

LISTENING TO YOUR LIFE: DAILY MEDITATIONS WITH FREDERICK BUECHNER. SAN FRANCISCO: HARPERSANFRANCISCO, **1992.**

Miscellany—*Listening to Your Life* is a daily devotional of 366 entries culled from Buechner's books. The hodgepodge collection works surprisingly well as a devotional and has been a favorite of Buechner aficionados.

Every Buechner book that had been published by 1992 is excerpted, with four exceptions: *A Long Day's Dying, The Seasons' Difference, The Return of Ansel Gibbs*, and *The Entrance to Porlock*. The editor even managed to squeeze a week's worth of devotional material out of *The Book of Bebb*.

THE CLOWN IN THE BELFRY: WRITINGS ON FAITH AND FICTION. SAN FRANCISCO: HARPERSANFRANCISCO, **1992.**

Preaching—This book has a place in my heart because it contains the meaningful essay "Adolescence and the Stewardship of Pain." It is another grab bag, and I'm classifying it under preaching because even though only six of its fourteen pieces are sermons, another four were first delivered orally on different occasions, meaning the great majority of this book was originally meant to be heard instead of read.

The Clown in the Belfry has not been kept in print, most probably because so much of it is available elsewhere. Large parts of it had already appeared in various publications before the book was printed, and nine of its fourteen pieces have been anthologized in *Secrets in the Dark*.

My affection for *The Clown in the Belfry* might be outsized, but it is quintessential, top-fifteen Buechner to me.

THE SON OF LAUGHTER. SAN FRANCISCO: HARPERSANFRANCISCO, 1993.

Novel—See chapter six.

THE LONGING FOR HOME: RECOLLECTIONS AND REFLECTIONS. SAN FRANCISCO: HARPERSANFRANCISCO, 1996.

Miscellany—Unlike *A Room Called Remember* or *The Clown in the Belfry*, its predecessors in the grab-bag department, *The Longing for Home* has a unifying theme. There are two sections, "The Home We Knew" and "The Home We Dream." Even with the theme, it is an impossible book to classify. The first sixty pages belong with the memoirs (some of it in the form of poems), and five sermons are included. A piece further expanding on Buechner's love for King Rinkitink of Oz appears, as well as four brief devotional pieces; a moving essay with some memoirish elements about wholeness; and a long essay about a house and mill in Shaftsbury, Vermont (down the road a bit from Buechner's place on Rupert Mountain), called "Of Whipples and Wheels," which is a historical piece unlike anything else in Buechner's opus.

Somehow, this grab bag works, maybe simply because home is such a powerful theme. The book is eloquent and melancholy, and it is required reading for those enchanted with the world of Frederick Buechner.

ON THE ROAD WITH THE ARCHANGEL. SAN FRANCISCO: HARPERSANFRANCISCO, 1997.

Novel—Like the other final novels of Buechner's career, *On the Road with the Archangel* was derived from an earlier source. In this case, Buechner has retold the apocryphal book of *Tobit*. The result is Buechner's happiest novel. As you read, you expect disaster to befall its innocent protagonists at any moment, but disaster never happens. Instead, the "great laughter" of faith is on full display. God—called the Holy One here—is good, and he intervenes in our world for good. People, of course, misunderstand the Holy One: "By and large the world believes in him for all the wrong reasons and . . . disbelieves in him for all the wrong reasons too."[19] But the Holy One is good, and this book is about his goodness.

Bidden or unbidden, God is present, the old saying goes, and that's the message here. *On the Road with the Archangel* is both gospel as comedy and gospel as fairy tale. God is in the business of making things right, loving his creation, and smiling and laughing with us as we discover his goodness.

THE STORM: A NOVEL. SAN FRANCISCO: HARPERSANFRANCISCO, 1998.

Novel—I concluded that Buechner's first novel, *A Long Day's Dying*, was ultimately about sin. Fittingly, *The Storm*, his last novel, published almost fifty years later, is ultimately about forgiveness. The book's characters parallel the characters in Shakespeare's final play, *The*

Tempest. In Shakespeare's play, a storm propels the story into action. In Buechner's book, a storm helps bring some resolution and reconciliation, although things are far from being neatly tied together.

I believe Buechner chose *The Tempest* as the inspiration for his final novel rather than his standby *King Lear* because *The Tempest* has a happy ending. Love or grace or God (although God is a fairly ambiguous character here) wins in *The Storm.*

The Storm isn't my favorite, but it still asks the same questions and holds the same tensions Buechner has worked with over the course of his career.

THE EYES OF THE HEART: A MEMOIR OF THE LOST AND FOUND. SAN FRANCISCO: HARPERSANFRANCISCO: 1999.

Memoir—See chapter four.

SPEAK WHAT WE FEEL (NOT WHAT WE OUGHT TO SAY): REFLECTIONS ON FAITH AND LITERATURE. SAN FRANCISCO: HARPERSANFRANCISCO, 2001.

Popular Theology—*Speak What We Feel* contains mini biographies of four of Buechner's favorite authors: Gerard Manley Hopkins, Mark Twain, G. K. Chesterton, and William Shakespeare as well as expositions of their finest work. Although I'm classifying this "popular theology," it's really "faith and literature"; while compelling, it doesn't feel like a traditional Buechner book until the four-and-a-half page afterword, when Buechner shifts into memoir mode and does what he does best. He writes with pathos, noting that he was ordained to do so many things, but all he's done is write: "If I make it as far as St. Peter's gate, the most I will be able to plead is my thirty-two books, and if that is not enough, I am lost."[20] Buechner knows as well as anyone that we are saved by grace, not our literary output, but that doesn't stop him from feeling blue.

The book's title comes from the closing lines of *King Lear*, when the Duke of Albany surveys the dead bodies littering the stage and says, "The weight of this sad time we must obey, / Speak what we feel, not what we ought to say." The sadness of their times was the crucible that Hopkins, Twain, Chesterton, and Shakespeare spoke their greatest work out of. Likewise, Buechner's greatest works, such as *Godric* and *Telling Secrets*, were formed from the crucible of his pain. Buechner has blessed countless numbers in the process; it is a mystery of God's grace that the particular story of one becomes a healing balm for so many. This is true of the four lives examined in *Speak What We Feel*, and especially true of the one doing the examining. This is another "almost" essential.

BEYOND WORDS: DAILY READINGS IN THE ABC'S OF FAITH. SAN FRANCISCO: HARPERSANFRANCISCO, 2004.

Popular Theology—*Beyond Words* takes the successful idea from *Listening to Your Life* and makes another daily devotional from Buechner's work. Like its predecessor, it also has 366 entries. This time, the book comes from Buechner's three lexical "ABC" books: *Wishful Thinking*, *Peculiar Treasures*, and *Whistling in the Dark*. Combining those three books produced a few entries with the same heading (some of which Buechner recycled under new names), and when all the content was added up, there was still a need for Buechner to write about two dozen new entries.

THE CHRISTMAS TIDE. NEW YORK: SEABURY, 2005.

Novel—*The Christmas Tide* is a reissue of *The Wizard's Tide* by a different publisher, with a different cover and a different title, hoping to reach a different audience. The only other difference is a short afterword by Buechner, in which he explains the rationale for

reissuing the book, hoping the new format and new title would help
the book reach his intended audience.

Secrets in the Dark: A Life in Sermons. San Francisco: HarperSanFrancisco, 2006.

Preaching—See chapter ten.

The Yellow Leaves: A Miscellany. Louisville: Westminster John Knox, 2008.

Miscellany—I was in the audience when Buechner debuted two of
the pieces in this collection at the inauguration of the Buechner Institute at King College (now University) in Tennessee. The hilarious
and tender first piece, "Our Last Drive Together," describes bringing
his mother one last time from visiting in Vermont to her apartment
in New York City. "Presidents I Have Known" (the title is a joke) tells
of brief but fascinating encounters with Franklin Roosevelt, Harry
Truman, and Dwight Eisenhower.

Buechner was shown tremendous appreciation that day at King.
There was sadness as he spoke of his difficulty writing and informed
us that this would be his final book. He was calling it *The Yellow
Leaves*, from Shakespeare's "Sonnet 73," because they were all that
remained on a tree that had once blossomed so productively.

The book is one last grab bag: the aforementioned pieces are
joined by several family poems, an essay about the year Buechner
spent abroad following the success of *A Long Day's Dying*, and even
a few pages of an abandoned novel focusing on a character from the
Bebb books. (He was apparently contemplating a fifth Bebb book!)

Shakespeare's sonnet refers to sweet birds that once sang, and
Buechner told us that day in Tennessee those sweet birds were no
longer singing. They do manage to get a few notes out on these pages,
and oh what memories we have of how they once did sing.

BUECHNER 101: ESSAYS AND SERMONS BY FREDERICK BUECHNER.
CAMBRIDGE, MA: BUECHNER CENTER, 2014.

Miscellany—This book was created and published by the Buechner
Center to introduce Buechner to new audiences. Anne Lamott wrote
an introduction; the tribute to Buechner that Barbara Brown Taylor
gave at the National Cathedral in 2006 is included; Brian McLaren's
foreword to *Secrets in the Dark* is reprinted; and Dale Brown provided an overview of Buechner's fiction.

Several Buechner books are also excerpted, providing glimpses of
Buechner's writing in several genres.

A CRAZY, HOLY GRACE: THE HEALING POWER OF PAIN
AND MEMORY. GRAND RAPIDS: ZONDERVAN, 2017.

Memoir—Two "new" Buechner books were released in the fall of
2017 containing previously unpublished Buechner work. This book
opens with a piece called "The Gates of Pain," which is an early draft
of "Adolescence and the Stewardship of Pain." Buechner speaks more
openly here than in his memoirs about his father's alcoholism and
his mother's difficult personality, and he identifies his oldest daughter,
Katherine, as the family member who had anorexia. The other essays
in this book were taken from previously published works such as *The
Sacred Journey, A Room Called Remember,* and *The Eyes of the Heart*
and are reprinted here because they unite around the theme of
healing through memory.

THE REMARKABLE ORDINARY: HOW TO STOP, LOOK,
AND LISTEN TO LIFE. GRAND RAPIDS: ZONDERVAN, 2017.

MEMOIR—This book consists entirely of previously unpublished material from a series of talks Buechner gave in 1987 and 1990. A lot of
it was reworked as the memoir *Telling Secrets.* I agree with the use of

the word *remarkable* in the title but don't think there is anything "ordinary" about the messages contained in this book. They aren't highly polished and refined—you get that in *Telling Secrets*—but the unvarnished Buechner is here, and this book especially contains important insights for those wanting to dig deeply into his psyche.

Notes

Foreword

[1]Fredrick Buechner, *The Longing for Home* (San Francisco: HarperSanFrancisco, 1996), 109.

Introduction: How Reading Buechner Changed My Life

[1]Frederick Buechner, *The Clown in the Belfry: Writings on Faith and Fiction* (San Francisco: HarperSanFrancisco, 1992), 87.

[2]Buechner, *Clown in the Belfry*, 96, 97.

[3]Buechner, *Clown in the Belfry*, 99.

[4]Frederick Buechner, *Now and Then* (New York: Harper & Row, 1983), 87.

1 *The Sacred Journey*: The Universal Particular

[1]Frederick Buechner, *The Remarkable Ordinary: How to Stop, Look, and Listen to Life* (Grand Rapids: Zondervan, 2017), 53.

[2]Frederick Buechner, *The Sacred Journey* (New York: Harper & Row, 1982), 6.

[3]Rebecca Solnit, *The Mother of All Questions* (Chicago: Haymarket, 2017), 19.

[4]Wallace Stevens, *The Necessary Angel: Essays on Reality and the Imagination* (New York: Alfred A. Knopf, 1951).

[5]Reynolds Price, "The Road to Devotion," *New York Times Book Review*, April 11, 1982, 11.

[6]Anne Lamott, ed., *Frederick Buechner 101: Essays, Excerpts, Sermons and Friends* (Cambridge, MA: Frederick Buechner Center, 2016), 1.

[7]Buechner, *Sacred Journey*, 1.

[8]John Calvin, *Institutes of the Christian Religion*, ed. John McNeill, trans. Ford Lewis Battles (Philadelphia: Westminster, 1955), 35.

[9]Buechner, *Sacred Journey*, 9.

[10]Frederick Buechner, *The Longing for Home: Recollections and Reflections* (San Francisco: HarperSanFrancisco, 1996), 12.

[11]Frederick Buechner, *The Wizard's Tide: A Story* (San Francisco: Harper & Row, 1990), 37.

[12]Frederick Buechner, *Telling Secrets* (San Francisco: HarperSanFrancisco, 1991), 73.

[13]Buechner, *Sacred Journey*, 14.

[14]Buechner, *Sacred Journey*, 46.

[15]Buechner, *Sacred Journey*, 3.

[16]Buechner, *Sacred Journey*, 72.

[17]Dale Brown, *The Book of Buechner: A Journey Through His Writings* (Louisville: Westminster John Knox, 2006), x.

[18]Frederick Buechner, *The Yellow Leaves* (Louisville: Westminster John Knox, 2008), 27.

[19]Buechner, *Sacred Journey*, 100.

[20]Buechner, *Yellow Leaves*, 45.

[21]"Briefly Noted, Fiction," *New Yorker*, January 5, 1952, 73.

[22]"Briefly Noted, Fiction," *New Yorker*, January 7, 1950, 79.

[23]Frederick Buechner, *The Alphabet of Grace* (New York: Seabury, 1980), 45.

[24]Buechner, *Sacred Journey*, 104.

[25]Buechner, *Sacred Journey*, 89.

[26]Frederick Buechner, *The Magnificent Defeat* (New York: Seabury, 1966), 48.

[27]Buechner, *Sacred Journey*, 109.

[28]Buechner, *Alphabet of Grace*, 44.

[29]See, for example, the discussion of the past, present, and future tenses of salvation in Darrell Guder, *Be My Witnesses* (Grand Rapids: Eerdmans, 1985), 83-88.

2 *NOW AND THEN:* FORREST GUMP'S FEATHER

[1]Frederick Buechner, *The Magnificent Defeat* (New York: Seabury, 1966), 60.

[2]Buechner, *Magnificent Defeat*, 91.

[3]Paul Tillich, *The New Being* (New York: Charles Scribner's Sons, 1955), 18.

[4]Muilenburg's story intersects mine. He was raised in the Reformed Church in America, the denomination in which I am ordained. He spent a year later in his career teaching at Western Theological Seminary, where I work. His brother was the longtime pastor of Westminster Presbyterian Church in Lansing, Michigan, and in addition to marrying my parents was one of my grandfather's best friends.

[5]Buechner, *Now and Then* (New York: Harper & Row, 1983), 15, 16.

[6]Buechner, *Now and Then*, 37.

[7]"Door Interview: Frederick Buechner," *Wittenburg Door*, December 1979–January 1980, 18.

[8]See, for example, W. Dale Brown, *Of Fiction and Faith: Twelve American Writers Talk About Their Vision and Work* (Grand Rapids: Eerdmans, 1997), 32-36.

[9]Frederick Buechner, *The Alphabet of Grace* (New York: Seabury, 1970), 40, 41.

[10]Frederick Buechner, *Secrets in the Dark* (San Francisco: HarperSanFrancisco, 2006), xiv.

[11]Buechner, *Secrets in the Dark*, xv.

[12]Brown, *Of Fiction and Faith*, 35.

[13]Harold Fickett, "A Conversation with Frederick Buechner," *Image Journal*, Spring 1989, 49.

[14]Frederick Buechner, *The Final Beast* (New York: Atheneum, 1965), 176-78.

[15]John Davenport, "Buechner's Fourth," *Spectator,* June 11, 1965, 763.

[16]Makoto Fujimura, *Culture Care: Reconnecting with Beauty for Our Common Life* (Downers Grove, IL: InterVarsity Press, 2017), 58.

[17]Frederick Buechner, *The Yellow Leaves* (Louisville: Westminster John Knox, 2008), 46.

[18]Brown, *Of Fiction and Faith*, 33.

[19]"Frederick Buechner Extended Interview," *Religion and Ethics Newsweekly*, May, 5, 2006, www.pbs.org/wnet/religionandethics/2006/05/05/may-5-2006-frederick-buechner-extended-interview/15358/.

[20]Buechner, *Alphabet of Grace*, 41.

[21]Karl Barth, *The Word of God and the Word of Man* (New York: Harper, 1957), 108.

[22]Buechner, *Now and Then*, 81.

[23]Buechner, *Now and Then*, 82.

[24]Buechner, *Now and Then*, 85.

[25]Buechner, *Now and Then*, 86.

[26]Buechner, *Now and Then*, 86.

[27]Buechner, *Alphabet of Grace*, vii.

[28]Buechner, *Now and Then*, 87.

[29]Buechner, *Now and Then*, 98.

[30]Buechner, *Now and Then*, 102.

3 *TELLING SECRETS:* A DEEPER HONESTY

[1]Frederick Buechner, *Telling Secrets* (San Francisco: HarperSanFrancisco, 1991), 7.

[2]Buechner, *Telling Secrets*, 10.

[3]Stephen Kendrick, "On Spiritual Autobiography: An Interview with Frederick Buechner," *The Christian Century*, October 14, 1992, 901.

[4]Buechner, *Telling Secrets*, 11.

[5]Buechner, *Telling Secrets*, 26, 27.

[6]Buechner, *Telling Secrets*, 28.

[7]See, for example, H.-L. Kantzer Komline, "Freedom, Free Will, and Determinism," in *Evangelical Dictionary of Theology*, ed. Daniel J. Treier and Walter A. Elwell (Grand Rapids: Baker Academic, 2017), 329.

[8]Jeremy Begbie, *Beholding the Glory: Incarnation Through the Arts* (London: Longman and Todd, 2000), 142-46.

[9]Leslie Weatherhead, *The Will of God* (Nashville: Abingdon, 1999).

[10]Buechner, *Telling Secrets*, 31.

[11]Russell Moore, "How Frederick Buechner Blessed My Life," *Christianity Today*, October 2017, 48.

[12]Buechner, *Telling Secrets*, 49.

[13]Buechner, *Telling Secrets*, 62.

[14]Buechner, *Telling Secrets*, 63.

[15]Buechner, *Telling Secrets*, 64.

[16]Buechner, *Telling Secrets*, 64.

[17]Buechner, *Telling Secrets*, 61, 62.

[18]Frederick Buechner, *The Magnificent Defeat* (New York: Seabury, 1966), 79.

[19]Buechner, *Telling Secrets*, 80.

[20]Buechner, *Telling Secrets*, 82.

[21]Buechner, *Telling Secrets*, 82.

[22]Frederick Buechner, *Whistling in the Dark: An ABC Theologized* (New York: Harper & Row, 1988), 5.

[23]Frederick Buechner, *Brendan: A Novel* (New York: Atheneum, 1987), 217. And curse the internet, which has this quote attributed to Brennan Manning in dozens of places.

[24]Buechner, *Telling Secrets*, 94, 95.

[25]Frederick Buechner, *The Longing for Home: Recollections and Reflections* (San Francisco: HarperSanFrancisco, 1996), 28.

[26]Buechner, *Telling Secrets*, 100.

[27]Buechner, *Telling Secrets*, 101.

4 THE EYES OF THE HEART:

REMEMBERING THE LOST AND FOUND

[1]Frederick Buechner, *The Eyes of the Heart: A Memoir of the Lost and Found* (San Francisco: HarperSanFrancisco, 1999), 1.

[2]Buechner, *Eyes of the Heart*, 11.

[3]Buechner, *Eyes of the Heart*, 1.

[4]Kastalia Medrano, "Where Do You Go When You Die? The Increasing Signs That Human Consciousness Remains After Death," *Newsweek,* February 10, 2018, www.newsweek.com/where-do-you-go-when-you-die-increasing-signs -human-consciousness-after-death-800443.

[5]Buechner, *Eyes of the Heart*, 12-13.

[6]Buechner, *Eyes of the Heart*, 14.

[7]Buechner, *Eyes of the Heart*, 15, 16.

[8]Buechner, *Eyes of the Heart*, 19, 20.

[9]Buechner, *Eyes of the Heart*, 23-24.

[10]Buechner, *Eyes of the Heart*, 60.

[11]Buechner, *Eyes of the Heart*, 60.

[12]Buechner, *Eyes of the Heart*, 61.

[13]Buechner, *Eyes of the Heart*, 62.

[14]Buechner, *Eyes of the Heart*, 44.

[15]Buechner, *Eyes of the Heart*, 45.

[16]Buechner, *Eyes of the Heart*, 38.

[17]Buechner, *Eyes of the Heart*, 31.

[18]Buechner, *Eyes of the Heart*, 31.

[19]Frederick Buechner, *A Long Day's Dying* (New York: Alfred A. Knopf, 1950), 228.

[20]Buechner, *Eyes of the Heart,* 39, 40.

[21]Buechner, *Eyes of the Heart*, 43.

[22]Buechner, *Eyes of the Heart*, 6.

[23]Buechner, *Eyes of the Heart*, 106.

[24]Buechner, *Eyes of the Heart*, 16.

[25]Thomas Long, "The Binary Christianity of Marcus Borg," *The Christian Century*, July 7, 2017, www.christiancentury.org/review/binary-christianity-of -marcus-borg.

[26]Marcus J. Borg, *Meeting Jesus Again for the First Time: The Historical Jesus and the Heart of Contemporary Faith* (San Francisco: HarperSanFrancisco, 1994), 17.

[27]Buechner, *Eyes of the Heart,* 87.

[28]Buechner, *Eyes of the Heart*, 91.

[29]Buechner, *Eyes of the Heart*, 161.

[30]Buechner, *Eyes of the Heart*, 163.

[31]Buechner, *Eyes of the Heart*, 180, 181.

[32]Buechner, *Eyes of the Heart*, 180.

[33]Frederick Buechner, *The Sacred Journey* (New York: Harper & Row, 1982), 112.

[34]Frederick Buechner, *Now and Then* (New York: Harper & Row, 1983), 109.

[35]Frederick Buechner, *Telling Secrets* (San Francisco: HarperSan Francisco, 1991), 106.

[36]Buechner, *Eyes of the Heart*, 183.

PART TWO: FREDERICK BUECHNER AS NOVELIST

[1]Kenneth Gibble, "Ordained to Write," *A.D.*, March 1983, 17.

[2]W. Dale Brown, "An Overview of Buechner's Fiction," in *Buechner 101: Essays and Sermons by Frederick Buechner*, ed. Anne Lamott (Cambridge, MA: Frederick Buechner Center, 2016), 120.

[3]Dale Brown, *The Book of Buechner: A Journey Through His Writings* (Louisville, KY: Westminster John Knox, 2006), 372.

[4]Maude McDaniel, "An Elusive Grace," *The World & I*, May 1999, 278-79.

[5]George Garrett, "The Character of Saints," *The World & I*, April 1993, 299.

5 *GODRIC:* A TWELFTH-CENTURY SINNER-SAINT

[1]Frederick Buechner, *Godric* (New York: Atheneum, 1980), 3.

[2]Buechner, *Godric*, 4.

[3]Buechner, *Now and Then* (New York: Harper & Row, 1983), 59.

[4]Buechner, *Godric*, 101.

[5]Frederick Buechner, *The Alphabet of Grace* (New York: Seabury, 1970), 47.

[6]Barbara Brown Taylor, *When God Is Silent* (Chicago: Cowley, 1998), 51.

[7]Robert G. Kemper, "Archaic Prose," *The Christian Century*, 98 (May 6, 1981): 524.

[8]Buechner, *Godric*, 62.

[9]Buechner, *Godric*, 167.

[10]Buechner, *Godric*, 17.

[11]Buechner, *Godric*, 85.

[12]Frederick Buechner, *Wishful Thinking: A Theological ABC* (New York: Harper & Row, 1973), 83.

[13]Frederick Buechner, *Wishful Thinking, A Seeker's ABC* (San Francisco: HarperSanFrancisco, 1993), 102.

[14]Frederick Buechner, *The Clown in the Belfry: Writings on Faith and Fiction* (San Francisco: HarperSanFrancisco, 1992), 18.

[15]Buechner, *Godric*, 20.

[16]Buechner, *Godric*, 105.

[17]"Buechner Tells the Truth," *The Falcon*, October 24, 1990, 5.

[18]Box 114, Series 5: Published Material. Frederick Buechner Papers, 1926-2010, Special Collections, Buswell Library, Wheaton College, Wheaton, IL.

[19]John Heaseley, "A Technicolor Saint Gets a Black and White Treatment," *Baltimore Sunday Sun*, November 2, 1980.

[20]Buechner, *Godric*, 31.

[21]Buechner, *Godric*, 44.

[22]Buechner, *Godric*, 4.

[23]Buechner, *Godric*, 174.

[24]Frederick Buechner, *Telling Secrets* (San Francisco: HarperSanFrancisco, 1991), 21.

[25]Buechner, *Telling Secrets*, 26-27.

[26]Buechner, *Godric*, 154.

[27]Buechner, *Godric*, 9.

[28]Buechner, *Godric*, 10-11.

[29]Buechner, *Telling Secrets*, 9.

[30]Buechner, *Godric*, 99.

[31]Buechner, *Now and Then*, 106.

[32]Buechner, *Clown in the Belfry*, 23.

[33]Buechner, *Now and Then*, 106.

[34]Dale Brown, *The Book of Buechner: A Journey Through His Writings* (Louisville: Westminster John Knox, 2006), 225.

[35]Frederick Buechner, *The Longing for Home: Recollections and Reflections* (San Francisco: HarperSanFrancisco, 1996), 28.

[36]Buechner, *Godric*, 96.

6 *THE SON OF LAUGHTER:* HEELS, LAUGHTER, AND THE FEAR

[1]Wendy Wise Herstein, "Never Beyond the Reach," *The World & I*, April 1993, 308.

[2]Michael D. Aeschliman, "Blessing and Bane," *The World & I*, April 1993, 302.

[3]Annie Dillard, "The Ancient Story of Jacob, Retold in a Passionate, Exalted Pitch," *Boston Sunday Globe*, May 30, 1993, A15.

[4]George Garrett, "The Character of Saints," *The World & I*, April 1993, 298.

[5]C. Frederick Buechner, "A Sermon," *Testament*, Fall 1990, 12-15.

[6]Herstein, "Never Beyond the Reach," 309.

[7]Frederick Buechner, *The Magnificent Defeat* (New York: Seabury, 1966), 18.

[8]Frederick Buechner, *Peculiar Treasures: A Biblical Who's Who* (New York: Harper & Row, 1979), 57.

[9]Frederick Buechner, *The Son of Laughter* (San Francisco: HarperSanFrancisco, 1993), 19.

[10]Buechner, *Son of Laughter*, 82.

[11]Buechner, *Son of Laughter*, 18.

[12]Buechner, *Son of Laughter*, 21.

[13]Buechner, *Son of Laughter*, 109.

[14]Buechner, *Son of Laughter*, 113, 114.

[15]Buechner, *Son of Laughter*, 94.

[16]Buechner, *Son of Laughter*, 159, 160.

[17]Walter Brueggemann, *Genesis: A Bible Commentary for Teaching and Preaching* (Atlanta: John Knox, 1982), 270.

[18]Brueggemann, *Genesis*, 271.

[19]Buechner, *Son of Laughter*, 166.

[20]Buechner, *Son of Laughter*, 86.

[21]Brueggemann, *Genesis*, 279.

[22]Buechner, *Son of Laughter*, 180.

[23]Buechner, *Son of Laughter*, 173.

[24]John F. Walvoord and Roy B. Zuck, eds., *The Bible Knowledge Commentary: An Exposition of the Scriptures by Dallas Seminary Faculty: Old Testament* (Wheaton, IL: Victor, 1986), 83.

[25]For example, see Susanne Scholz, "What 'Really' Happened to Dinah: A Feminist Analysis of Genesis 34," *Lectio Difficilior* 2 (2001), www.lectio.unibe.ch/01_2/s.htm.

[26]Talitha J. Arnold, "Telling Secrets, Telling the Truth," *Reflections,* Winter-Spring 1982, 22.

[27]Frederick Buechner, *Secrets in the Dark: A Life in Sermons* (San Francisco: HarperSanFrancisco, 2006), 289.

[28]Frederick Buechner, *The Seasons' Difference* (New York: Alfred A. Knopf, 1952), 15.

[29]Kenneth Gibble, "Listening to My Life: An Interview with Frederick Buechner," *The Christian Century*, November 16, 1983, 1043-44.

PART THREE: FREDERICK BUECHNER AS POPULAR THEOLOGIAN

[1]Frederick Buechner, *Wishful Thinking: A Seeker's ABC* (San Francisco: HarperSanFrancisco, 1993), 112.

7 *Wishful Thinking:* Renewing Tired Words

[1]Philip Yancey, "The Reverend of Oz," *Books and Culture,* March/April 1997, 7-8.

[2]"Door Interview: Frederick Buechner," *Wittenburg Door,* December 1979–January 1980, 18.

[3]Frederick Buechner, *The Magnificent Defeat* (New York: Seabury, 1966), 111.

[4]Frederick Buechner, *Wishful Thinking: A Seeker's ABC* (San Francisco: HarperSanFrancisco, 1993), 23, 24, 36, 65, 119.

[5]Yancey, "Reverend of Oz," 9.

[6]Frederick Buechner, *Wishful Thinking: A Theological ABC* (New York: Harper & Row, 1973), 67.

[7]Frederick Buechner, *Wishful Thinking: A Seeker's ABC*, 81.

[8]Frederick Buechner, *Now and Then* (New York: Harper & Row, 1983), 13.

[9]Paul Tillich, *Systematic Theology* (Chicago: University of Chicago Press, 1951), 1:237.

[10]Charles Marsh, *Strange Glory: A Life of Dietrich Bonhoeffer* (New York: Alfred A. Knopf, 2014), 450.

[11]Russell Moore, "How Frederick Buechner Blessed My Life," *Christianity Today,* October 2017, 46.

[12]Harold Fickett, "A Conversation with Frederick Buechner," *Image Journal,* Spring, 1989, 52.

[13]Buechner, *Wishful Thinking: A Seeker's ABC*, 108, 109.

[14]Buechner, *Wishful Thinking: A Seeker's ABC*, 95.

[15]Paul Tillich, *Dynamics of Faith* (New York: Harper & Row, 1957), 18.

[16]Buechner, *Wishful Thinking: A Seeker's ABC*, 30.

[17]Buechner, *Wishful Thinking: A Seeker's ABC*, 102.

[18]Buechner, *Wishful Thinking: A Seeker's ABC*, 77.

[19]Fickett, "Conversation with Frederick Buechner," 52.

[20]"Letters," *A.D.*, June 1973, 77.

[21]"Letters," *A.D.*, June 1973, 77.

[22]"Letters," *A.D.*, June 1973, 52.

[23]Buechner, *Wishful Thinking: A Seeker's ABC*, 30, 31 .

[24]Frederick Buechner, *Whistling in the Dark: A Doubter's Dictionary* (San Francisco: HarperSanFrancisco, 1993), 12, 13.

[25]Frederick Buechner, *The Book of Bebb* (New York: Atheneum, 1979), 143.

[26]Yancey, "Reverend of Oz," 7, 8.

[27]Lauren Winner, "The Doubter's Library," *re:generation quarterly* 6, no. 1, Spring 2000.

[28]"Door Interview: Frederick Buechner," 18.

[29]Russell Moore, "How Frederick Buechner Blessed My Life," *Christianity Today*, October 2017, 46.

[30]Buechner, *Wishful Thinking: A Seeker's ABC*, 87.

[31]Frederick Buechner, *Peculiar Treasures: A Biblical Who's Who* (New York: Harper & Row, 1979), 13.

[32]"Door Interview: Frederick Buechner," 20.

[33]Jack Buckley and Sharon Gallagher, "A Conscious Remembering: An Interview with Frederick Buechner," *Radix*, July/August 1983, 8.

[34]Buechner, *Magnificent Defeat*, 65.

[35]Buechner, *Wishful Thinking: A Seeker's ABC*, 46.

[36]Buechner, *Wishful Thinking: A Seeker's ABC*, 26, 27, 72.

8 *PECULIAR TREASURES:* PEOPLE WE THOUGHT WE KNEW

[1]Jill P. Baumgaertner, *Flannery O'Connor: A Proper Scaring* (Chicago: Cornerstone, 1988), ix.

[2]Frederick Buechner, *Now and Then* (New York: Harper & Row, 1983), 95.

[3]Jack Buckley and Sharon Gallagher, "A Conscious Remembering: An Interview with Frederick Buechner," *Radix*, July/August 1983, 6.

[4]Father Joris, OFM, "'Vulgar' vs. 'Official' Christian Language," *National Catholic Reporter*, June 29, 1979; Margaret B. Spittler, "Peculiar Treasures,"*Chattanooga Daily Times*, July 1, 1979.

[5]Box 115, Series 5: Published Material. Frederick Buechner Papers, 1926-2010, Special Collections, Buswell Library, Wheaton College, Wheaton, IL.

[6]Frederick Buechner, *Peculiar Treasures* (San Francisco: Harper & Row, 1979), 2-3.

[7]Buechner, *Peculiar Treasures*, 74.

[8]Buechner, *Peculiar Treasures*, 8.

[9]Buechner, *Peculiar Treasures*, 78.

[10]Buechner, *Peculiar Treasures*, 14.

[11]Buechner, *Peculiar Treasures*, 6.

[12]Buechner, *Peculiar Treasures*, 64.

[13]Buechner, *Peculiar Treasures*, 68-69.

[14]Frederick Buechner, "All's Lost, All's Found," *The Christian Century*, March 12, 1980, 284.

[15]Buechner, *Peculiar Treasures*, 83.

[16]Buechner, *Peculiar Treasures*, 181-82.

[17]Buechner, *Peculiar Treasures*, 179.

[18]Buechner, *Peculiar Treasures*, author's note, xi.

9 *TELLING THE TRUTH:* TEARS WITH GREAT LAUGHTER

[1]Frederick Buechner, *Telling the Truth: The Gospel as Tragedy, Comedy, and Fairy Tale* (New York: Harper & Row, 1977), 13.

[2]Buechner, *Telling the Truth*, 14.

[3]Anne Lamott, ed., *Buechner 101: Essays and Sermons by Frederick Buechner* (Cambridge, MA: Frederick Buechner Center, 2016), 19.

[4]Leonard Allen, "Almost Poetry," *Christian Century*, May 16, 1979, 570.

[5]Herman Ridder, "Hilarious Sermonizing," *The Church Herald*, July 13, 1979, 15.

[6]Buechner, *Telling the Truth*, 14.

[7]Buechner, *Telling the Truth*, 23. In chapter six I noted the criticism made by Talitha J. Arnold in a 1982 article of the gender-exclusive nature of the references in *Telling the Truth*. Buechner changed to an inclusive style later, but *Telling the Truth* has never been updated since its 1977 release.

[8]See my reference to *Open Heart* in the appendix.

[9]Buechner, *Telling the Truth*, 33.

[10]Buechner, *Telling the Truth*, 38.

[11]Buechner, *Telling the Truth*, 39.

[12]Buechner, *Telling the Truth*, 41.

[13]"Frederick Buechner Extended Interview," *Religion and Ethics Newsweekly*, May 5, 2006, www.pbs.org/wnet/religionandethics/2006/05/05/may-5-2006-frederick -buechner-extended-interview/15358/.

[14]Frederick Buechner, *Wishful Thinking: A Seeker's ABC* (San Francisco: Harper-SanFrancisco, 1993), 29.

[15]Buechner, *Telling the Truth*, 56.

[16]Buechner, *Telling the Truth*, 58.

[17]Buechner, *Telling the Truth*, 60.

[18]Buechner, *Telling the Truth*, 63.

[19]Buechner, *Telling the Truth*, 64.

[20]Buechner, *Telling the Truth*, 65.

[21]J. R. R Tolkien, *The Tolkien Reader* (New York: Ballantine, 1966), 68.

[22]Buechner, *Telling the Truth*, 78.

[23]Buechner, *Telling the Truth*, 83.

[24]Buechner, *Telling the Truth*, 90, 91.

[25]Buechner, *Telling the Truth*, 91.

[26]Buechner, *Telling the Truth*, 90.

[27]Buechner, *Telling the Truth*, 95.

[28]Buechner, *Telling the Truth*, 95.

[29]Buechner, *Telling the Truth*, 92.
[30]Buechner, *Telling the Truth*, 96.

10 *SECRETS IN THE DARK:* THE WONDER OF WORDS

[1]Donald Wilson Stake, "Conversation with Frederick Buechner 'On Preaching,'" *Reformed Liturgy & Music*, Spring 1994, 60, 61.

[2]Frederick Buechner, *Secrets in the Dark: A Life in Sermons* (San Francisco: Harper-SanFrancisco, 2006), 16.

[3]Buechner, *Secrets in the Dark*, 19.

[4]Buechner, *Secrets in the Dark*, 71.

[5]Buechner, *Secrets in the Dark*, 260.

[6]Molly Collins Phelps and Rob Collins, producers, *Buechner* (New Life Films, 2007).

[7]Frederick Buechner, *The Longing for Home: Recollections and Reflections* (San Francisco: HarperSanFrancisco, 1996), 170.

[8]Buechner, *Secrets in the Dark*, 164.

[9]Buechner, *Secrets in the Dark*, 167.

[10]Buechner, *Secrets in the Dark*, 240.

[11]Buechner, *Secrets in the Dark*, 159.

[12]Buechner, *Secrets in the Dark*, 2.

[13]Buechner, *Secrets in the Dark*, 8.

[14]Buechner, *Secrets in the Dark*, 51.

[15]Buechner, *Secrets in the Dark*, 273.

[16]Buechner, *Secrets in the Dark*, 274.

[17]Buechner, *Secrets in the Dark*, 275.

[18]Buechner, *Secrets in the Dark*, 276, 277.

[19]Buechner, *Secrets in the Dark*, 278.

[20]Frederick Buechner, *Whistling in the Dark: A Doubter's Dictionary* (San Francisco: HarperSanFrancisco, 1993), 15-17.

[21]Buechner, *Secrets in the Dark*, 255.

[22]Buechner, *Secrets in the Dark*, 255.

[23]Buechner, *Secrets in the Dark*, 254.

11 READING BUECHNER TODAY

[1]W. Dale Brown, *Of Fiction and Faith: Twelve American Writers Talk About Their Vision and Work* (Grand Rapids: Eerdmans, 1997), 33.

[2]Frederick Buechner, *Now and Then* (New York: Harper & Row, 1983), 14.

[3]Frederick Buechner, *The Final Beast* (New York: Atheneum, 1965), 178.

[4]Frederick Buechner, *The Remarkable Ordinary: How to Stop, Look, and Listen to Life* (Grand Rapids: Zondervan, 2017), 62.

[5]Philip Yancey, *Soul Survivor: How My Faith Survived the Church* (New York: Doubleday, 2001), 248.

[6]Yancey, *Soul Survivor*, 248.

[7]Yancey, *Soul Survivor*, 269.

[8]Russell Moore, "How Frederick Buechner Blessed My Life," *Christianity Today*, October 2017, 46, 48.

[9]George Garrett, "The Character of Saints," *The World & I*, April 1993, 299.

APPENDIX: AN ANNOTATED BIBLIOGRAPHY OF FREDERICK BUECHNER'S BOOKS

[1]Frederick Buechner, *A Long Day's Dying* (New York: Alfred A. Knopf, 1950), 54.

[2]Buechner, *Long Day's Dying*, 3.

[3]Frederick Buechner, *The Seasons' Difference* (New York: Alfred A. Knopf, 1952), 275.

[4]Buechner, *Seasons' Difference*, 221.

[5]George P. Winship Jr., "Mission to Novelists," *The Christian Century*, January 18, 1956, 75, 76. Ironically, Winship taught English at King College in Bristol, Tennessee, where the Buechner Institute was founded fifty years after this article appeared.

[6]Eugene Peterson, *Take and Read: Spiritual Reading—An Annotated List* (Grand Rapids: Eerdmans, 1996), 63.

[7]Frederick Buechner, *The Hungering Dark* (New York: Seabury, 1968), 31.

[8]Frederick Buechner, *Wishful Thinking: A Seeker's ABC* (San Francisco: Harper-SanFrancisco, 1993), 119.

[9]Buechner, *Hungering Dark*, 35-36.

[10]Frederick Buechner, *The Entrance to Porlock* (New York: Atheneum, 1970), 257.

[11]Frederick Buechner, *Now and Then* (New York: Harper & Row, 1983), 100.

[12]Frederick Buechner, *The Book of Bebb* (New York: Atheneum, 1979), 147.

[13]Buechner, *Book of Bebb*, 177-79.

[14]Roger Sale, "Review of *Love Feast*," *Hudson Review*, Winter 1974, 635.

[15]Buechner, *Book of Bebb*, 389.

[16]Buechner, *Book of Bebb*, 447.

[17]Buechner, *Book of Bebb*, 501.

[18]Buechner, *Book of Bebb*, ix.

[19]Buechner, *On the Road with the Archangel* (San Francisco: HarperSanFrancisco, 1997), 108.

[20]Frederick Buechner, *Speak What We Feel (Not What We Ought to Say)* (San Francisco: HarperSanFrancisco, 2001), 160.

INDEX